Benefits of
Vaastu
&
Feng Shui

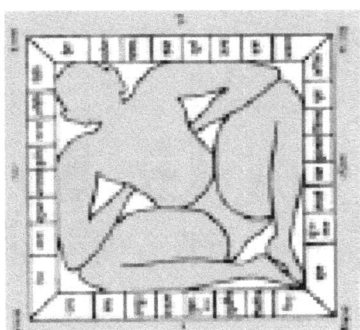

Rajendar Menen

Published by:

F-2/16, Ansari Road, Daryaganj, New Delhi-110002
☎ 011-23240026, 011-23240027 • *Fax:* 011-23240028
Email: info@vspublishers.com • *Website:* www.vspublishers.com

Regional Office : Hyderabad
5-1-707/1, Brij Bhawan (Beside Central Bank of India Lane)
Bank Street, Koti, Hyderabad - 500 095
☎ 040-24737290
E-mail: vspublishershyd@gmail.com

Branch Office : Mumbai
Jaywant Industrial Estate, 2nd Floor-222, Tardeo Road
Opposite Sobo Central, Mumbai - 400 034
☎ 022-23510736
E-mail: vspublishersmum@gmail.com

Follow us on:

All books available at **www.vspublishers.com**

© Copyright: *V&S PUBLISHERS*
ISBN 978-93-813845-3-4
Edition 2016

The Copyright of this book, as well as all matter contained herein (including illustrations) rests with the Publishers. No person shall copy the name of the book, its title design, matter and illustrations in any form and in any language, totally or partially or in any distorted form. Anybody doing so shall face legal action and will be responsible for damages.

Printed at : Param Offseters, Okhla, New Delhi

DEDICATION

MAY GOOD VAASTU AND FENG SHUI GUIDE
ALL THE GODDESSES WHO BROKE BREAD
WITH ME ALONG THE WAY.

Acknowledgement

There are billions of words on Vaastu and Feng Shui. There are also several score practitioners and theorists who have taken great pains in their interpretation of these sciences. We would like to specially acknowledge the contributions of Wendy Hobson and Juliet Pegrum, among others. They have taken enormous effort to explain the complexities in everyday language.

Contents

Acknowledgement	......	*iv*
Preface	......	*vii*

Section I : Vaastu Shastra

Vaastu and the Home	......	10
Guidelines for City Living	......	28
Workplace Rules	......	31
The Vaastu of Cities	......	36

Section II : Feng Shui

Origins of Feng Shui	......	40
Understanding the Basics	......	50
Mystical Belief or Natural Science?	......	60
The Question of Consultation	......	68
Landscaping and the Elements	......	73
The Significance of Yin and Yang	......	79
Early History of Qimancy	......	86

Section III : The Various Elements in Feng Shui

More Hints for Protection	......	94
Feng Shui in the Workplace	......	104
Understanding the Trigrams	......	110
Activating the Energies in Your Home	......	117

Section IV : Energising the Home

Using Feng Shui in the Home	......	124
The Kua Number	......	134
Feng Shui in the Garden	......	137
Glossary	......	142

Preface

Vaastu and Feng Shui are household names today. Suddenly, almost out of nowhere, like an ancient prophecy come alive, they have emerged out of the closet and taken the world by storm. Both have ancient origins. Both have been conceived in the womb of two of the most ancient civilisations in the world; Vaastu is Indian and Feng Shui is Chinese in origin. And both have many similarities and one end: to make life happier, healthier and more prosperous for those who follow the principles.

There are hundreds of thousands of books, websites, shops and outlets all over the world selling Feng Shui and Vaastu information and merchandise. Practitioners have become well-known newspaper columnists and merchandise has travelled to homes across the globe.

The twenty-first century has seen many new developments. The world has now woken up to the immense possibilities of maximising the human potential. Man has realised that with the right diet, the right exercise, the right medication and the right environment, he can give his life a longer and more fruitful lease. Vaastu and Feng Shui fall squarely into this paradigm of evolution, growth and betterment.

Writing a book on Vaastu and Feng Shui is not easy. There are several complexities that need to be unravelled and a lot depends on the interpretation of the practitioner. However, a strong thread of common sense runs through both, and that helps. While there are millions of words on the subject, Wendy Hobson and Juliet Pegrum were illuminating in their interpretation of the subject.

We hope this book helps you understand the science

better as we have dealt a lot on the origins. We also hope that it stirs your curiosity to know more about the subject and make effective changes in your everyday life. The idea simply is to help you fulfil your potential in every way and lead a happier, healthier and more prosperous life.

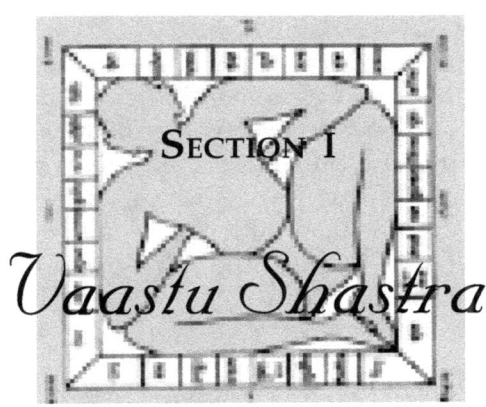

Section I
Vaastu Shastra

Vaastu and the Home

"Let the everlasting air and light make comfortable the house that is built up with skill and knowledge and measured and erected by learned architects."

–**Atharva Veda**

Among the oldest literary works known to man written around 2500 BC, the Vedas mention gods directly related to *Vaastu Vidya* (knowledge of Vaastu). The Hindu triad of Brahma, Vishnu and Shiva and their wives are important to Vaastu. Lakshmi, wife of Vishnu, is the Goddess of Fortune and she attracts wealth. Saraswati, wife of Brahma, is the Goddess of Science and Wisdom. Of course, the most popular Indian deity is Lord Ganesh, the son of Shiva and Parvati.

In the Hindu pantheon of gods and goddesses, Shiva is the creator and destroyer. He is depicted with a blue throat and his sacred animal is Nandi, the bull. He has four arms, usually holding a bow, a club, a drum and a noose. His symbol is the *lingam* or phallus, which emerges from the female *yoni*.

Vishnu has ten major incarnations: Matsya, Kurma, Varcha, Narasimha, Vamana, Parsurama, Rama, Krishna, Buddha and Kalki. He is depicted with his consort, Lakshmi, resting on a lotus. His sacred animal is Garuda, which is half man, half bird.

Brahma is the symbol of creation connected with the origin of the universe. He has four faces of which only three are visible. They represent the four Vedas. His four hands denote the four directions and hold a rosary, water pot, book, sceptre, spoon, bow or lotus. The swan is his vehicle.

Ganesh, perhaps the most popular Indian god, has an elephant's head, four to ten arms, and a round belly. His vehicle is a rat and he holds a rope, an axe, a goad and a dish of sweetmeats. The fourth hand is in the boon-giving position. Lord Ganesh is the destroyer of obstacles and is also known as the God of Wisdom.

Vaastu Vidya is ancient Indian knowledge. The word *Vaastu* means *to dwell* and *Vidya* means *science* and so, quite literally, Vaastu Vidya is the sacred science related to designing and building houses. Vaastu is rooted in Vedic philosophy and is considered by experts and practitioners to be the distant ancestor of Feng Shui, the Chinese art of geomancy, which we will be elaborating later in this book.

Both Vaastu and Feng Shui have the same goals – to restore the balance between the home and the cosmos bringing health, wealth and happiness to those who follow the principles, most of which are based on simple common sense. There may be an esoteric element to the science but it rests a lot on the interpretation of the practitioner one is consulting.

Vaastu believes that the external and the internal are interchangeable. According to Vaastu, the energies that govern the elements, like wind or fire, are similar to those that control the organs of the human body. According to Vaastu, when buildings echo the underlying cosmic principles, they vibrate in harmony with the universe. These vibrations also affect those who are housed in the building and can determine their health, wealth, happiness, progeny and prosperity.

Following Cosmic Principles

Vaastu aims to realign the home with cosmic principles. Its approach is holistic. Its principles are ancient, yet it is unconditioned by time, country, climate or geography. Initially, it was carefully guarded but the principles gradually spread by word of mouth.

According to Vaastu, energy lines run like a large grid across the earth, from north to south and from east to west. The electromagnetic field generated affects the human body at the cellular level. Vaastu also uses the cardinal directions. The sun rises in the east ushering the day and represents beginnings; the setting sun in the west is an indicator of endings; the north is where the pole star is and denotes stability and security; and the south represents the past.

Vaastu emphasises the right proportions. It focuses on a plan for any form, be it a room or a building. The plan used in Vaastu is the *Vaastu Purusha Mandala*, which is a three-dimensional *yantra* containing all the forces acting on any given space.

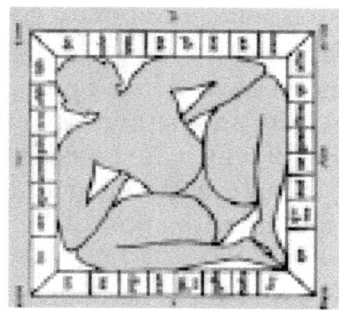

Purusha is symbolised as a man with his stomach facing the earth. He is the embodiment of all the cosmic forces. When his image is laid across any area under the consideration of Vaastu, his head is positioned towards the north-east. It is then believed that this area becomes the body of Purusha. From the Mandala that is prepared, any working and living situation can be properly aligned. The Mandala is in the form of a square with eight compass directions. Vaastu believes that if *prana* or cosmic energy is proper in the environment, there will be happiness, health, prosperity and harmony.

In India, it is generally believed that Vaastu Purusha exists in every home. His head rests in the north-east and the feet and folded legs in the south-west. Offerings to the Goddess of Wealth are placed at his head and his heart is considered vulnerable and so heavy furniture is never positioned on it.

According to Vaastu, the movement of energy through a four-sided structure is similar to the energy that flows through the earth. Therefore, the home should mirror the earth and be designed accordingly. Vaastu believes that the movement of *prana*, within a house or apartment, flows from the north-east and meanders towards the south-east and north-west corners before heading to the south-west. The Vaastu Purusha, as we have already mentioned, looks down on the earth with his body aligned to the north-east/south-west axis and his head in the north-east. His head indicates the direction in which positive pranic energy enters a house.

In the traditional concept of Vaastu, the layout of a house and the corresponding functions of each room have been prescribed according to the position of the sun throughout the day. Accordingly, the period between three and six in the morning, just before sunrise, is called *Brahma Muhurta*. This is the time when the sun is in the north-eastern section of the house. This is a good time for meditation. From six to nine in the morning, the sun is in the eastern part of the house. This is a good time for bathing; and the east is logically a good location for the bathroom.

From nine in the morning to noon, the sun is in the south-east part of the house. It is a good time to eat, and the direction is a good location for the kitchen. This is also a good time for preparing food as well as to eat. Between twelve and three in the afternoon is the resting period and the sun is in the south, which is an ideal location for a bedroom. Between three and six in the evening, the sun is in the south-west section of the house. This is a good location for a study.

The evening, between six and nine, is a good time for eating. The sun is in the west, which is a good location for a dining room. The period between twelve and three in the morning, when the sun is in the north, is the time for secrecy, rest and sleep.

Ancient Origins

It should be remembered that the principles of Vaastu are applicable to space of any scale. Ancient India was very different from the India of today. When Vaastu was born thousands of years ago, India was agrarian and urban sprawls as we see today were non-existent. There were no big cities and India was lost in a time warp with snakes, elephants, kings and peasantry dotting a beautiful, unsullied and vast landscape. Natural and man-made calamities were frequent. The sophistry and technology that we see today were not even a distant dream. Vaastu happened at that time. But its principles were so solid, meaningful and profound that they hold good even today in the din, chaos, pollution and restricted spaces of Indian cities.

In Vaastu, the size of the space doesn't matter; whatever the area, the same principles apply. Vaastu practitioners normally use a compass to determine magnetic north. In Vaastu, true north is the direction towards the North Pole.

The first step, of course, is in choosing the site. Vaastu starts from the road and so the nature of a site can be determined by the direction of the road or roads that border it. When two roads border the property, it is important that the corners of these sites are neither rounded nor cut across. Mentioned below are types of sites with their attributes and disadvantages.

It is believed that a site with a road to the south can cause problems especially if the road is at a lower level than the house. But if the road is to the west, blocking the north and east, it is considered neutral. If the road lies to the east of the property, it is a positive location, as the morning sun will penetrate the site. When the road runs to the north of the property it is good, particularly if the north side is unobstructed for the free flow of cosmic energy.

When there is a road to the south and a road to the east, it is referred to as a south-eastern site, which is also considered good. A north-eastern site is one that has two roads bordering it, one to the north and one to the east. It is considered good in Vaastu if the two roads are lower than the property or on the same level. A north-western site, where one road is in the west and another in the north, is considered neutral.

In Vaastu, the surrounding landscape and the shape of the site are also taken into consideration. The square and rectangle are considered the perfect shapes in which to dwell as they have the most beneficial energy fields. Irregular shapes are best avoided unless they extend towards the north-east. Triangular sites are the worst as these are associated with Agni or fire.

It is preferable if the site is flat. A hill to the south or west of a building is fine but if the hill is on the north-east side, sunlight can be blocked. Water is always a good sign, although it is ideal if it flows from the south or the west towards the east or the north.

Commonsense Approach

Some common sense here – Vaastu emphatically points out that it is best to avoid buildings near burial grounds. Also, if roads surround the home, it may be difficult to live without a feeling of insecurity, as there will be a continuous flow of traffic. It is also preferable if the building is not overshadowed by larger structures like a flyover or a large tree.

In Vaastu, it is preferable to have some space between houses. In the bigger cities of India, space is a problem and so there is enormous pressure on the flow of light, ventilation and cosmic energy. A garden, however small, is welcome as it encourages the movement of *prana*. Indoor gardens are also useful in the crowded, apartment-style living of our urban sprawls, but we will come to that later. A dwelling with a garden is much better than a house that opens directly to the street. The garden should be a square or a rectangle and it is preferred if there isn't a tree in the front garden taller than the house.

Normally, when there are rows of houses, one row will attract all the positive influences while the houses on the opposite side of the street will attract all the negative energies. When there are rows of houses, the row that faces north acquires all the benefits, while the one that faces south is left with the negative influences. West-facing houses remain neutral while east-facing houses are positive. When rows of houses are opposite one another, it is important to avoid gates and doors which are in direct alignment.

Circumventing Space Constraints

As we mentioned earlier, it is all very easy to talk about space and how houses should face a certain direction and not another. All that is possible with the luxury of space. But in the densely populated cities of the world and in India, where the bigger cities are an unimaginable mess, space is the first casualty. Even the trees are counted, the open spaces are jammed with hawkers and the jogging trails crammed with those trying to fill their lungs with healthy oxygen. Space is limited and the cost exorbitant. So in cities like Mumbai, for example, where people are choked in high-rise apartments and slums, space acquires a different connotation altogether.

But all this doesn't deter Vaastu. Its principles, though ancient, hold good even today. In Vaastu each apartment, however small, is looked upon as an independent unit. If one lives in an apartment block, it is advisable to choose the first floor or higher to avoid the negative influences at ground level. If the entire block is square or rectangular, there is a stronger connection with the earth. As per the principles of Vaastu, square buildings are considered masculine while rectangular buildings are feminine and softer. If the apartment is on the north, north-east or east side of the block, it will receive positively charged morning light.

The apartment block should have sufficient space around it and should be well ventilated to allow natural light to enter all the rooms. It should also not be overshadowed by larger buildings.

As per the traditions of Vaastu, there are also strict guidelines for the use of building materials in construction. The purists believed that every substance has a living energy; some are positive and others are negative. Sandstone and marble have a positive influence while granite and quartz can create health problems. They also insisted that glass and reinforced concrete should not be used for construction purposes.

In Vaastu, rocks and trees are thought to have age and gender. The stone used in construction should be mature and should vibrate with a deep sound when struck. Practitioners of Vaastu believe that concrete is a dead material and emits a negative energy. It is also against the use of steel, glass and other synthetic material.

According to Vaastu, the square is the perfect shape in which to live. This principle applies to all spaces irrespective of its size. The square represents the universe in microcosm and is considered strong and stable. But if one is making extensions, then certain principles of Vaastu can be adhered to. The preferable shape for an extension is either a square or a rectangle. Extensions in the north-east section of the property are considered positive. South of south-east and west of north-west are also positive directions for extensions.

The gate is also of great importance in Vaastu. Apart from the right first impressions, it also influences the overall atmosphere of the place. The position of the front door in relation to the gate is also significant. It is preferable to have the front door facing the same direction as the gate. It is also good for the house to be located to the left of the gate. But it is considered unlucky to have the house on the right side when entering the gate.

Guidelines for Doors

Vaastu also insists on the avoidance of obstructions near the house as they restrict the flow of energy. If there is a tree close to the front gate, a ditch, a lamppost or any such obstruction, it is not considered auspicious. Of course, all this is easier said than done as our cities are filled with obstructions of all sorts. In such cases, a little distance between the door and the obstruction is recommended. The purists are also not in favour of a road pointing directly towards the property. The gate should not be in direct alignment with the road.

After opening the gate, the path to the front door of the house also has a great impact on the flow of energy to the house. If the path lies to the north-east, it should be broader and more open at the gate and become narrower as it approaches the house. If the path is in the south-east, it is better if it is of the same width throughout.

According to the principles of Vaastu, the front door is considered to be the mouth of Purusha and should be the largest door in the house. A single front door is better if it faces north or east with steps leading up to it. It is considered catastrophic if the front door is placed in the centre of a wall. The door should ideally face the north-east corner, and if the front door faces south or west, it is better to have it at ground level. Doors of different houses should not be directly opposite one another.

The size of the door should also be proportionate to the house. Proportion is very important in Vedic architecture. If the height of the front door is equal to the width, it conveys peace; if the height is one and a quarter times the width, it transmits strength and emanates wealth, but the door that is approximately thrice the width is considered to be the best.

The door should also open smoothly and shouldn't swing unnecessarily. If it makes a tuneful sound, it is considered positive. But squeaking doors are not considered good. Tearful sounds are also bad. It is ideal if the front door is made of wood and not of metal, which is saturnine in influence. The front door should also open to a welcoming and pleasant sight. In the same vein, pleasant sights should greet you when you open the door to leave the house. Vaastu Shastra lays a lot of focus on the position of doors and entrances, their proportions and obstructions.

Rituals for a New Home

Since all living spaces are said to be filled with unseen entities, the purification of the place is mandatory before its occupation. So certain rituals or pujas are conducted. The first is performed before the construction actually commences, the second on positioning the main door, the third to ensure that the new occupants have happy lives, and the fourth set of rituals are associated with moving in.

Before entering a new home a Vaastu puja is performed to the imaginary Vaastu Purusha. The place is scrupulously cleaned and a light is carried to the centre of the house where a jug of water, white flowers and burning incense have already been placed. Milk is then boiled until it overflows or food is cooked and offered to the gods. Then follows a prayer for health, wealth and happiness.

Finally, holy water mixed with sandalwood oil is sprinkled into each corner of the property to purify it. The food that has been cooked is then offered to the gods and given to the guests as *prasad*.

There are five essential items required for a puja: water or milk, incense, flowers, a light and a bell. The water or milk represents the element water, the incense is symbolic of the element air, the flower represents earth, the light symbolises fire and the sound of the bell represents space. In this manner, all the elements are brought together and offered to the gods of the space directions to ensure the protection and prosperity of the home.

The Role of Colours

Colours have a powerful impact on us. This has also been proved scientifically. Heliotherapy, or the use of sunlight in the treatment of diseases, has been in use for a long time. Sunlight is apparently pure white light, though it is a combination of the seven colours of the rainbow. Each colour has an independent vibration that affects the mind and the body and activates human glands.

In Vaastu, colours play an important role. They are linked with the three *gunas*: *sattva*, *rajas* and *tamas*. Blue, green, white and light colours are considered sattvic. Rajasic colours are fiery reds, oranges and pinks. The tamasic colours are browns and black.

Colours can influence the size and shape of a room. Light colours give the illusion of space. Softer, more sattvic colours promote harmony, red increases desire, blue and green are cooling and yellow stimulates cerebral activities. Violet, which enhances introspection, is best in the meditation room, and a baby's room should ideally be bright.

Interestingly, the colour of the front door should be in harmony with the direction it faces. A door facing north should be a shade of blue, for example.

Location of the Kitchen

The kitchen is a very important location in Vaastu Shastra. Cooking is a major ritual in India and enormous amount of time is normally spent in the kitchen, as it is where nourishment is provided to the entire family. For maximum benefit, the kitchen should be located in the south-east section of the house and as far away from the front door as possible. The kitchen should be well ventilated and should be on the ground floor in a multi-storeyed house and preferably never on a higher floor.

The south-east is the corner that corresponds to the element fire. The *guna* rajas predominates this area of the house. The north-west is also governed by rajas and is okay, but the north-east corner is certainly to be avoided. Since it is believed that the food being prepared will absorb the energy of the direction one is facing, one should face east while preparing food. Facing south-west will disturb the harmony of the house, facing west will cause health problems and facing north will invite financial losses.

The sink should be placed in the north-east section of the kitchen. The fridge and the storage cupboards are best arranged along the southern and western walls, and ovens or microwaves should be placed in the south-east section.

According to Vaastu, the dining area is best located in the west. It is preferable to have a separate dining area, not too far from the kitchen but certainly away from the toilet and the front door. The dining table should be rectangular and it is best to face east or west while eating. The walls should be painted a soft, calming colour, either light blue or green and the environment should be conducive to good eating. Paintings of fruits in the dining room symbolise abundance.

The living room can occupy any direction as long as part of it occupies the centre of the house, which is the area that receives the least amount of cosmic energy and so is ideal for relaxation. But according to Vaastu practitioners, a good direction for the living room is the west or the north. The west is the exalted position of Mercury and helps promote memory and intelligence. Jupiter, the planet of learning and study, influences the north.

It is also best to place heavy furniture like sofas and chairs in the south or the west. While seated, it is best to face east or north. The telephone can be placed either in the south-east or the north-west, and family photographs should be in the south-west corner. The television can be located along the east wall. The living room should be painted in calming colours.

Importance of Proper Lighting

Light is an important element and is represented by the sattva *guna*. The sattva corner of a property is the north-east, which represents creative, positive energy. So natural light from the north-east is preferable. Natural light is a powerful source of energy and one can indulge in a little excess here. Lighting can change the atmosphere of a room. If light fittings are positioned along the north and east walls, it is positive, but light from the south-east corner is not considered all that good. Dark rooms and corridors can be brought to life with good interior lighting.

Many aspects of Vaastu Shastra lie in the domain of common sense and a good interior decorator can easily make a house look beautiful and well ventilated with a lot of free flowing energy all around. Exquisite lighting is also well in the ambit of good interior decoration.

In Vaastu Shastra, great importance is laid on creating a secure environment for sleep. Good rest, the ancients realised, was essential for the well-being of the body and mind and a proper time and place was allotted for it. According to ancient rishis, certain locations are more conducive to peaceful sleep than others. The direction in which one sleeps is also important. There is a correlation between the magnetic field of the earth and the human body, which is like a magnetic pole with the head corresponding to the North Pole. As per guidelines in the *shastras*, it is best to sleep with the head towards the east or the south and never the north, as the two similar poles will repel each other and create chronic health problems.

The master bedroom, it is said, should be one of the largest rooms in the house. It should be located in the south-west where it receives the least light. It is also the area associated with the element earth, which is stable and inactive and therefore provides restful conditions for sleep. A room in the west or south sides of the house is also fine for a bedroom. This is applicable even in small living areas like one-room apartments, which are so common in our big cities. Just make sure that the sleeping area is in the south-west corner of the room. In multi-storey houses, the bedroom should be on the first floor or higher and preferably not on the ground floor.

Vaastu also details the proportions and design of the bed. It should be of good quality wood and not metal, which is associated with Saturn and so can be cold and saturnine. The headboard should have flower or leaf motifs and should be kept clean and tidy. Soft bedsheets and fragrant flowers add to making it a comfort zone where one can indulge in sleep and other sensual pleasures. The bed should be in the south-west corner of the room. Other heavy furniture should be kept in the south or the west side of the bedroom. The dressing table should be kept along the north wall and the mirrors along the north or east walls only.

The walls can be painted with soft, light tones at the red end of the colour spectrum, as red is a good colour to enhance feelings of love and warmth.

What's Best for Children

The best location for a child's room is the east side of the house. The east side of the house is influenced by the energy of sattva, which supports new life and growth. Children have a different energy from adults and need the active energy of rajas, which is also available in the north-west side of the house.

The child's bed should be positioned along the south or west walls and the child should ideally face the east. The west and the south should be avoided. Computers and televisions in a child's bedroom can interfere with sleep and so it is a good idea to avoid them. Excessive colours can also be avoided as this can lead to over-stimulation. Children are, in any case, boisterous and full of energy and, if anything, they need a restful atmosphere.

Bedrooms, in general, should not be positioned over areas like the garage or basements, which have a lot of restless energy and are not conducive for sleep. For guests who come and go, the guest bedroom can be in the north-west, which is ruled by the energy of rajas and causes restlessness. This is fine for a guest room because none of the occupants will be there permanently. But this is certainly not the ideal venue for the master bedroom of the house, which calls for permanence.

Other Commonsense Measures

Fresh flowers, aired, well-ventilated rooms, light colours on the walls, a minimum of electrical equipment in the room as they interfere with sleep, ditto with mirrors directly over the bed, are a few of the suggestions for general well-being and harmony. Curtains to protect the room from the noises and lights of the street and keeping the bed away from doors and windows to protect from draughts are other commonsense measures. If electrical equipment like computers cannot be shifted, they should at least be covered. Heavy furniture can be placed along the south and west walls, and in the guest room the visitor's head can be positioned towards the east, south and even west though it is not a long-term solution.

In ancient India, the bathroom and toilet were placed outside, away from the house. One had to walk a distance and also use separate footwear placed there for the purpose. If the palaces, for instance, had bathrooms, it was located in the south-west of the building or in the genital area of Vaastu Purusha. Bedrooms with attached bathrooms, so much in vogue these days, were not common in those days. Of course, space is a major consideration now.

In Vaastu, it is preferable to have two separate rooms for sleeping and bathing to ensure that the energy of neither room is disturbed. Both rooms have different functions, different energies and, therefore, different identities. The north-west is also a good location for a bathroom as it is the water area of the house. A bathroom without a toilet is fine in the east.

The bathroom is ruled by the moon and should be kept clean. Mirrors along the north and east walls are fine by Vaastu. The toilet should not be too close to the kitchen for obvious reasons. According to the principles of Vaastu, the toilet should be installed along the north-south line so that when you are seated you face north. Light colours in the bathroom are refreshing.

Nature Around the House

Gardens or nature in and around the house are very important in Vaastu. There is a profound connection between man and nature. So it is necessary to have indoor and potted plants even in tiny urban apartments and feel connected to the natural world. The colour green is also important to rebalance ourselves after the hectic urban whirl our lives have become.

If your house has a garden, it should either be square or rectangular. Irregular shapes are best avoided. If the garden is irregular, then square the corners. Landscaping is essential in such cases, as the irregular corners have to be squared. It is also necessary to check the soil and the vegetation already growing. It should be smooth and not too acidic or alkaline.

Some thumb rules: make sure there are no thorny shrubs, as this will keep prosperity from the house, and avoid a property with trees that are close by and taller than it. The south-west side is ideal for large trees and bushes, while small plants or a lawn can be on the north-east side. This way there will be a supply of pure oxygen as well as protection from the rays of the afternoon sun.

If there is a pond in the house, it is best placed in the north-east section. Gold fish and water lilies enhance the quality of the pond. Trees, if any, should be on the south and west borders of the garden. Flowering trees and fragrant flowers provide the most uplifting vibrations.

Some more tips: rock gardens should be in the south-west corner and if there is a barbecue it should be in the south-east or fire corner. What is important is that *prana* or life force should flow unencumbered. It is the lifeblood of the environment and contributes immensely to well-being.

In Vaastu Shastra, boundary walls are important. They define the parameters of a property and the flow of energy in and out of the home. To promote harmony and to prevent negative energies from entering the house, it is necessary to have well-maintained fences. The saying, 'Good fences make good neighbours', while rooted in common sense, is echoed in the principles of Vaastu.

The ideal shape of one's property should be either a square or a rectangle with all the corners at right angles.

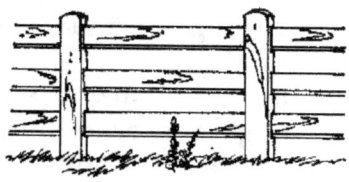

The perfect measurements in Vaastu are for the height of the outer walls to be three-quarters the height of the front door. The walls along the south and the west should be about a foot higher than the north and east walls. Vaastu says the south and west walls should be thicker and slightly higher than the north and east walls.

Vertical fences are considered more effective than those that are horizontally spaced. The north-east side of the property can have open horizontal fencing or if there is a wall on the north and east sides, then openings along it are advisable to allow the free flow of energy. Brick walls are good on the south and west sides of the property. They help keep out negative forces and encourage good *prana*.

But there are exceptions to all the rules. For example, if the gradient of the land slopes from the north to the south or the west to the east, then a wall needn't have vents.

ooo

Guidelines for City Living

Space is a big problem in the bigger cities of the world, particularly in India. Even tiny, one-room apartments in cities like Mumbai are at a premium and can cost the earth. But space can be carefully and intelligently broken up into several compartments for different functions. If it is a one-room apartment, it is better if it is not on the ground floor or in the basement, as it will attract the vibrations of the street, the garden and the passers-by and can not only be noisy but also distracting.

Heavy furniture and storage units should be kept along the south and west walls. In a one-room apartment it is imperative to optimise space. Every inch is precious. A clever architect can devise fold-aways and storage units, which don't intrude into the existing space.

The level of the floor in the south-west section can also be raised making it heavier and higher. If a mezzanine floor is created, it should be located along the south or west walls only. The kitchen should be in the south-east or the north-west corner of the room and while cooking one should face east. The bathroom should be situated in the east, south-west or north-west. One-room apartments with the bathroom in the north-east will only drain finances. The north-east corner should have no heavy furniture and should be kept open and the centre of the room shouldn't be cluttered with heavy furniture.

In cities like Mumbai, one-room apartments also double up as office spaces. So space has to be very carefully arranged. The television or computer can be placed towards the south-east of the room, which is the fire corner. Since space is at a premium, it is imperative to keep it clean and free from clutter. This prevents stagnant energies from accumulating. It isn't easy to throw away things as we get attached to them and feel that even items currently of little use can be put to good use later. It is important to remember that clutter focused on a particular area of a room will affect the corresponding area of one's life. To give an example, clutter in the northern section will obstruct the flow of prosperity. All spaces have energy. The idea is to enhance it, not deplete it.

Nearly all homes have pictures and paintings on the walls. But many people are unaware that they can have a profound effect on the home or the workplace. In Indian philosophy they evoke *rasas* or strong sentiments. There are nine *rasas* in all covering the whole spectrum of human emotions: *Shingara* is seductive, induced by beauty; *Hasya* is comic; *Karuna* is pathetic; *Roudra* brings anger; *Vira* is heroic; *Bhayanaka* is fearful; *Adbhuta* is the feeling of amazement; *Biphasta* is the feeling of repulsion; and *Sahanta* is peaceful and meditative. The *rasas* that are suitable are *shingara, hasya* and *sahanta*. So a combination of seductive, comic and peaceful images is ideal for the home. Images should be uplifting, positive, harmonious and generate feelings of growth, abundance and love. Fearful scenes like bloody battles, wounded animals and gore should be avoided, as they do nothing for the vibrations of the space.

Vaastu also talks about where pictures are to be hung. Images of fruits and flowers symbolise vitality and are best hung on the east or north walls. Pictures of wealth should be hung on the north wall, landscapes depicting mountains should be hung on the south and west walls and landscapes with rivers and lakes should be on the north and east walls.

Images of carnivorous animals should never be hung. Horses, cows and elephants, which symbolise strength, abundance and success, are good to hang on the walls.

Bloody battles, barren landscapes and similar images are best avoided. Simply put, all the images that hang on the walls should evoke peace, joy, happiness and success. Harsh images give out harsh vibrations. The essence is to uplift the ambience in every manner possible.

The roof of a building is also significant in Vaastu. Its shape, its slope and other details can influence those who inhabit the dwelling. If the roof slopes, it should be even on both sides. If the slope is irregular, it should be more towards the north or the east and less towards the south or the west. Chimneys, if any, should be on the south or west sides. Overhead water tanks are best placed on the south or west of the building and never on the north-east, as it will obstruct the flow of prosperity. Roof terraces are best on the north or the east of the building.

Television aerials and satellite dishes are best connected on the south-east section of the building, which is the fire corner. Telephone lines and outside lights are also best kept on the south-east side of the property. Drainage water from the roof should also be arranged in such a way that the water flows from the south and west and runs off the north or east side of the building. Skylights, if any, should be located on the north or east sides of the roof.

Living in basements is not recommended in Vaastu as it can cause mental instability. Underground car parks in apartment blocks, quite common now, will create a lot of restless energy in the building. Most modern buildings have one and in that case the north-east corner of the parking lot should be left empty. Cellars should be located on the north or east sides of the property. The stairs leading to the basement should slope from the south or west and heavy items of furniture which are stored in the basement are best kept along the south and west walls. A generator or boiler in the cellar is best placed in the south-east corner.

Underground spaces, without question, affect the energy of the building. But the rule to be observed is that the land should be even or slope from the south or west towards the north or east.

ooo

Workplace Rules

The workplace is a very good area to put the principles of Vaastu into use. The same principles apply to both residential and commercial spaces touched, of course, with a lot of common sense, which we see running through all the principles of Vaastu. All over the world, there are some businesses that flourish and some that just don't. Look at even shopping malls close to your place. Some shops do fabulously well and others are more or less empty all the time. There must be a solid reason for this as success in any enterprise is a combination of several factors.

One of the most important factors in business is the right location. If one is dealing in a fast-moving, low shelf life item of everyday need, the bustling marketplace is the best location. At another level, businesses involving medicines need to have a strong north-east aspect, which is supposed to charge the medicines with natural *prana*. Other office spaces are ideal in the central business district of a city or town, as the vibrations and the facilities available will be most suitable.

In a large office space, the different departments have to be carefully placed with the principles of Vaastu in mind. The physical and emotional needs of all staff members have to be taken into consideration to optimise their potential. Even if one works from home, which is quite the norm these days in the bigger cities, it is necessary to have a specially designated area for this purpose. For research or study, the best part of the home to work in is the north. For other work needs, the south-west area is fine. But if the bedroom and the office are in the same space, it is best to place the bed in the south-west corner and the desk in the north-east corner of the room.

The work desk should face east or north. The desk should be made of wood or marble and it should be so placed that it faces an extended space in front and not a wall.

Then the usual commonsense measures: windows behind are unnerving and a good seat with good back support optimises work potential. The area should be kept clean and free from litter to prevent the accumulation of stagnant energy. Filing cabinets to the south-west, electrical equipment in the south-east and the waste paper basket in the south-west are the other recommendations. Indoor water fountains in the north-east along with images of wealth on the north or east walls, freshly-cut flowers for the right fragrance and shades of yellow to stimulate the mind are some more useful tips. The whole idea is to keep the room fresh, clean, fragrant and symbolic of abundance and prosperity.

While choosing office space, it is best to avoid complexes built of reinforced concrete or those that contain too much metal. Taller buildings or flyovers should not overshadow the property. It is preferable if the building is either square or rectangular. The main entrance to the office should be in the north-east, south of south-east or west of north-west. There should be no obstructions and the door should open easily without a squeak in accompaniment. The building should also have easy access. A car park, if any, should ideally be situated west or south of the premises and the gradient of land surrounding the building should be level or higher on the south or west side.

The reception area should ideally be in the north-east corner. It should also be at the lowest point with steps, staircase or a lift leading to the rest of the company. The reception desk itself should be positioned in the south or west corner of the room and the receptionist should face north or east. The back should be against the wall and the computer should be kept on the south-east section of the main reception desk.

The reception area is not a profit centre and so normally a lot of emphasis is not placed on it. But it is a very important area. It is the receiving zone for business and is the first impression of the office for a visitor. It should present the outsider or first-time guest with the right vibrations and set the tone for the rest of the office. Courtesy, friendliness and warmth in the reception area mean a lot to a stranger entering the office for the first time. With the right touches, the reception centre can also be the harbinger of profits. Many embellishments can be made too: natural light and proper ventilation, soft music, indoor fountains, aquariums, the right artificial lights, appropriate furnishing and so on.

The managing director of the company is equal to the head of the household. So his office corresponds to the master bedroom and should be one of the largest rooms situated in the south-west corner of the building. The principles of Vaastu lay great emphasis on the direction faced while working. It explains that if one faces east while working, there will be peaceful thoughts, the south-east induces drowsiness, the south encourages a devious mind, the south-west an aggravated mind, while the west is good for play. The north-west incites thoughts of travel and restlessness, the north is good for spiritual development and the north-east can make one otherworldly.

The ideal entrance to the office should be in the north-east. The desk should be in the south or west of the room and one should face east or north towards the doorway. It is good to have a wall behind rather than a door or window. Book shelves should be along the south or west walls and a drinks cabinet in the south-east corner of the room. A safe can be kept along the north wall.

In large organisations with various departments, the right location is of paramount importance. General administration is best positioned in either the west or south of the building on either side of the managing director's office. It is best if staff face north or east and so the desks should be positioned to enable that. The accounts department should be in the north of the building. All heavy equipment like safes or filing cabinets should be placed in the south or west.

The refreshment area in the office corresponds to the kitchen of the house. So it should be located in the south-east or the north-west. Water dispensers should be located in the north-east section of individual offices, while a canteen or restaurant is best located in the west. It is also best to face east or west while eating and so appropriate care should be taken to position chairs correctly.

Any heavy machinery should be kept either in the south or the west of the building and heavy items like desks and cabinets should be positioned in the south-west of individual rooms. Equipment relating to fire should be placed in the south-east. Wastepaper baskets should be placed in the south or west of the office and never in the north. Waste products, if any, should be disposed of in the south or west of the premises. Products that need storage should be kept in the south-west and products that need to be dispatched must be in the north-west of the office as the direction has a transitory energy. The north-east is ideal for a reception area.

The bathroom and toilet area in an office are best located in the south-west corner, which is the genital area of Vaastu Purusha. The north-west is also okay. For reasons of privacy and hygiene, the bathroom should be positioned away from the office and have a separate entrance. Avoid the north-east for a bathroom as it can cause a drain on finances. The ladies bathroom can be positioned in the south-east corner. Showers can be located in the east and the toilets in the south and west of the room. The toilets should be so placed that the person who uses them faces north or east. Since the moon influences bathrooms, reflective surfaces like mirrors can be used.

Most modern offices have an open-plan model. There are individual workstations in an open room. However, according to Vaastu, there are many negatives to this. People have different energies, personalities and work styles. Some are team players, others work best in privacy. An open office can have many distracting energies and certain cubicles will have a more positive energy than others. To provide an example, the person in the north-west will suffer from restlessness and may not stay long with the company. There will be a high turnover of those occupying a seat in the north-west direction.

The modern office concept should instead have more flexibility and the employee should be given the option of facing a direction of choice. Movable screens will provide the necessary privacy and help control the flow of light. The workstations should be positioned more towards the south-west of the room and leaving the north-east clear.

Then, of course, follow the commonsense dictates which closely accompany Vaastu: use comfortable seating, soft music, anoint the area with fresh flowers and plants, allow as much natural lighting as possible to flow in and, where necessary, tasteful indoor lighting can be used.

ooo

The Vaastu of Cities

All over the world, most thriving cities are located near water. Manhattan, one of the world's most well-known urban landscapes, is surrounded by water. The Hudson River is on one side and the East River on the other. The flow of water is predominantly from the north-west to the south-east. However, because the water also flows from the north to the south, it also indicates that prosperity flows out of New York.

The island is oriented along the north-east and south-west axes and so activities related to these areas are the main preoccupation for most New Yorkers. The south-east is the kitchen area and so eating out is big in New York. A depleted north-west encourages restlessness, which probably also contributes to the transient nature of New York. The south-west is connected to business and ancestry and this is where the thriving financial district is located. Ellis Island in the south-west is where the immigrants first entered America and so there is a strong connection to the island's ancestry.

The north-east is the direction of the arts and learning, and New York is and has been filled with thinkers and reformers of all kinds with a surfeit of cultural events adorning the ethos of a bubbly, buzzing city.

The centre of New York, the *Brahma bindu*, has been left open with Central Park, the wide-open lung of the city. Obviously, Vaastu is at work in New York too. Is this by intent or accident?

Tirupati's Vaastu

Tirupati in the southern state of Andhra Pradesh is the abode of Lord Venkateshwara, the Lord of Wealth. It is arguably India's most popular *devasthanam* or place of pilgrimage, and a special destination for those seeking favours from the Lord. It is considered the richest temple in India and is said to receive over 100,000 pilgrims every day and over Rs.5 billion in donations every year.

Tirupati is also well known all over the world, thanks to the large number of Indian immigrants everywhere. Its claim to fame also lies in the tonsuring of human heads that happens in the hundreds of thousands every year. It is a common sight for a visitor or pilgrim to Tirupati to see tonsured heads every inch of the way!

There are three main temples: Tiruchanur, Tirupati, and Tirumala. Tiruchanur is the gateway to Tirupati, next to the Swarnamukhi River. Tirupati is situated on the plains between the river and the mountains and is the largest temple complex. The shrine of Lord Venkateshwara at Tirumala temple lies on a hill, which is part of the Eastern Ghats. This is the heart of Tirupati. Paths lead to it from all directions and the climb can be arduous. There are buses, taxis and every form of transport plying in plenty, but there are many who also make the difficult climb on foot, on all fours and even on their knees to appease the Lord or in answer to a prayer granted. Tirumala is the oldest temple at Tirupati and was built in the mid-twelfth century during the culturally rich Chola period. The temple was built with the principles of Vaastu as a place of unconditional surrender to the larger powers that decide the destiny of the world.

The temple is set lower than the surrounding hills. The highest peak is to the south-west of the temple and the lowest towards the east. The ground slopes from the west to the east and there is an abundance of water in the area, which also flows from the west to the east. The temple entrances face east and the main building lies in a south-westerly direction. The mandapam on the south-east has been raised and is higher than the north-east. The kitchen is positioned in the south-east corner. The inner sanctum is of perfect proportions and the main shrine faces east.

Despite many military takeovers and kings losing to other kings in battle in the chequered history of south India, the temple has continued to prosper. According to those in the know, it is a simple case of Vaastu at work.

"Vaastu contains the hidden key to realigning the home with cosmic principles such as solar energy, the movement of the celestial spheres, the magnetic field of the earth, gravity, and the influence of the moon and sun. It offers a holistic approach to the design and layout of houses. Although the principles of Vaastu are constrained by ancient universal laws, they are unconditioned by time and remain as relevant today as they were 4,500 years ago. The traditional wisdom of Vaastu is not easily deciphered from original texts; instead the ancestral secrets have been passed by word of mouth from master to disciple," says Juliet Pegrum, who has contributed immensely to the understanding of Vaastu through her invaluable book *The Vaastu Vidya Handbook*.

Pegrum adds, "The science of Vaastu is complete in itself and, if properly applied, will ensure happiness in worldly life. It offers a vision of the supreme truth of the energies lying behind all phenomena, reconnecting humankind to the environment and to our true nature."

> *A refuge art thou, O house with broad roof and stores full of good clean grain. May at evening the calf and the young son enter your gates with a stream of cattle when they return home.*
>
> *This dwelling built with worship, designed by the wise, may Indra and Agni, the gods immortal, preserve the house, the seat of Soma.*
>
> *May all thy directions, to eastward, southward, northward, and westward, receive me graciously whenever I go about them. May I never fall down when standing on thee!*
>
> **–Atharva Veda**

We will now look at Feng Shui and its applications.

ooo

Section II

Feng Shui

Origins of Feng Shui

From the ancient Indian science of Vaastu Shastra, let us now take a look at Chinese Feng Shui. *Feng Shui* (pronounced *phong schway*), meaning *wind and water*, is practised worldwide. It is an ancient and mystical Chinese art and has been in use for thousands of years.

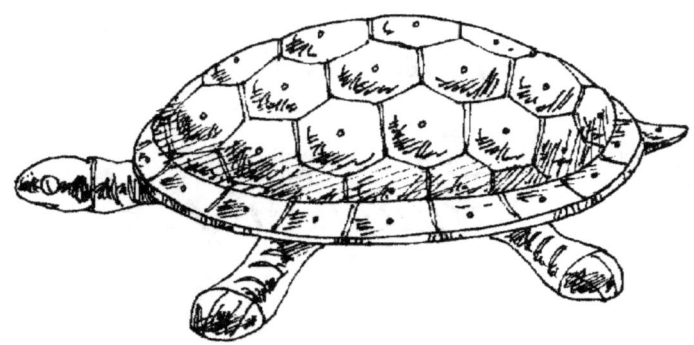

According to legend, the sage Fu His, who lived more than three thousand years ago, saw a turtle, the Chinese symbol of lifelong happiness, climb out of a river in spate. The sage (who was meditating on the banks of the river) noticed that the patterns on the shell of the turtle were arranged in groups of numbers which created the *lo shu* or magic square – a square in which all the numbers add up to fifteen in any direction. He believed that there are eight major types of energy in nature in addition to *tai chi*, the source and focus of all energies. The patterns on the turtle shell also had nine divisions, and so he concluded that these related to the same types of energy, which were, in fact, pervading everything in the universe. He allocated a Trigram – a symbolic group of three lines that illustrates the Yin/Yang balance – to each of the energies except *tai chi*.

He then applied the principle that everything in the universe related to the same types of energy. He also developed the *I Ching*, the Chinese book of changes. Feng Shui is built on these foundations. Literally meaning *wind and water*, it aims to bring about harmony in nature. Simply interpreted, harmony in nature is harmony in life.

In the beginning, the emperors of China zealously guarded the principles of Feng Shui. They wanted it preserved within the precincts of royalty. They used the principles in the location and arrangement of their palaces as well as the gravesites of their ancestors.

However, the secret could not be kept a secret for too long. The aristocracy soon got wind of it, after which the general population also got to know about the uses of Feng Shui. From China, Feng Shui spread all over the world. Now it is a household name, almost akin to a global brand. There are countless books on the subject, innumerable practitioners, and Feng Shui stores and shops by the thousands, as a whole new lexicon has entered the fabric of our everyday life.

All this has also given birth to an array of critics and cynics. But observe the principles closely and you will see that a lot of it is built on sheer common sense. Of course, Feng Shui, quite like its Indian counterpart Vaastu, is also rooted in many complexities, which can only be unravelled by a qualified practitioner. But like Vaastu, it also has a thread of common sense running through it.

Feng Shui is all about simplicity. Its aim is really very basic: to restore the natural balance in oneself and in one's surroundings and help create favourable energy around the home to establish the right environment for improving every aspect of one's life.

Feng Shui attempts to stimulate one of the three kinds of good fortune. According to the Chinese we are influenced by *tien chai* or heaven luck, which we are born with. Our earth luck is *ti chai*, which Feng Shui attempts to improve. But it has to be supported by *ren chai*, which is the luck one creates on earth, the luck that happens when opportunities are seized since life, as we all know, is all about making the most of half chances.

Since Feng Shui is all about bringing about harmony, it is used to decide the right place to erect houses, buildings or cities that will conform to the shape of the land and help people live in harmony with the environment. Practitioners say topographical formations, which are called 'dragons' or 'tigers', should not be disturbed and structures should not interfere with the flow of *sheng chi* or the life breath, a force that controls our destiny.

"Feng Shui is related to the very sensible notion that living *with* rather than *against* nature benefits both humans and our environment. It is also related to the equally sensible notion that our lives are deeply affected by our physical and emotional environs. If we surround ourselves with symbols of death, contempt and indifference toward life and nature, with noise and various forms of ugliness, we will corrupt ourselves in the process. If we surround ourselves with beauty, gentleness, kindness, sympathy, music and various expressions of the sweetness of life, we ennoble ourselves as well as our environment," says Robert Todd Carroll, a philosophy teacher at Sacramento City College in California.

What is *Chi*?

It is very important to understand the concept of *chi* to fully comprehend Feng Shui. It is sometimes translated as the *breath of life* or the *dragon's breath*. It is a subtle flow of electromagnetic energy and permeates everything in the universe. The three kinds of luck are related to the three basic kinds of *chi*. *Tien chi* is governed by the heavens, *ti chi* is contained in the veins of the earth and *ren chi* moves between the heaven and the earth. According to the Chinese, the earth is the body of the dragon and the streams and waterways are the dragon's blood. They carry *chi* around the universe.

As we have already explained, Feng Shui means *wind and water*. Water or *shui* sustains life. The movement of air or *feng* acts as a carrier for water. Both are essential for survival. To find the most auspicious environment in which to live, one has to identify the place where *ti chi* is the best. This only means that we reassess our environment and take measures to optimise the benefits. This is the form school of Feng Shui.

Chi is supposedly found in all things. It is said to be the vital force that breathes life into plants, animals and man, and inflates the earth to form hills and mountains. Since human *chi* is affected by atmospheric *chi*, Feng Shui experts make sure both don't clash to prevent bad luck or misfortune.

"No changes are made to the shape and appearance of the landscape that might disturb locally the harmonious flow of the earth's vital energy. More than that (a Feng Shui expert) may actually improve the landscape, manifesting its latent powers and making the pattern of its energy field conform more closely to the ideal requirements of its inhabitants. This he does by judicious setting of all buildings, tombs, walls and roads, with the addition of pillars, temples and monuments at the spots designated by nature to receive this," says John Mitchell, a British antiquarian who has written extensively about Feng Shui.

How Practical is Feng Shui?

A lot of Feng Shui is simple and built around common sense. For instance, Feng Shui tells us that a canal or river at the back of the house is bad. This is understandable because if the waterway is not cleaned, you could have a problem with disease-carrying mosquitoes or a foul stench, which could be just as bad.

Also considered unlucky is a house beside an overpass. This also makes a lot of common sense. Other no-nos are a house located on the site of a former cemetery or funeral parlour and one with a floor level lower than the main road. Again, one doesn't need to stretch one's imagination to realise how sensible these suggestions are.

But Feng Shui also attracts innumerable charlatans. According to William L. Cassidy of the Tibetan Medical and Astrological Institute in India, "Feng Shui has become corrupted to contain absurd notions of interior decoration, the use of charms and talismans, and the runaway concept of 'site' improvement, by several generations of practitioners who know nothing of its true essence. There are scores of people who cater to popular superstition, offering to decorate homes, 'improve' new businesses or resolve neighbourhood conflicts, all for a hefty fee. Recent (and popular) English and Chinese language books on the subject have just compounded the problem."

How Expensive is Feng Shui?

It depends a lot on the practitioner, his knowledge and his perception. Many apartments and offices have been broken down and rebuilt according to the Feng Shui practitioner's dictates.

For a couple contemplating Feng Shui, the cost of converting their home to attract good *chi* can be enormous, not to mention the fact that it can be inconvenient. Many apartments lose or gain value according to the Feng Shui practitioner's evaluation.

This is what happened in the early part of Chinese history where Feng Shui almost stopped the modernisation of that country. The English missionary E.J. Eitel described the problem in 1873 this way: "When purchasing a site, when building a house, when pulling down a wall, or raising a flagstaff, residents in the Treaty Ports have encountered innumerable difficulties and all on account of Feng Shui. When it was proposed to erect a few telephone poles, when the construction of a railway was urged upon the Chinese government, when a mere tramway was suggested to utilise the coal mines of the interior, Chinese officials would invariably make a polite bow and declare the thing was impossible on account of Feng Shui.

"When the Hong Kong government cut a road, now known as the Gap, to the Happy Valley, the Chinese community was thrown into a state of abject terror and fright, on account of the disturbance which this amputation of the dragon's limbs would cause to the Feng Shui of Hong Kong.... When Senhor Amaral, the governor of Macao – who combined a great passion for constructing roads with an unlimited contempt for Feng Shui – interfered with the situation and aspects of Chinese tombs, he was waylaid by the Chinese, his head cut off, and the Chinese called this the revenge of Feng Shui."

Today's practitioners thankfully do not resort to these desperate moves, though they are making a killing of a different kind in the New Age marketplace. But if you are planning to improve your home, a good architect or interior decorator may well be able to infuse the right Feng Shui.

A Historical Perspective

According to Dr Stephen L. Field of Trinity University, a scholar of traditional Chinese thought, Feng Shui is as old as Chinese culture itself (Neolithic Yangshao villages date from about 6000 BCE). According to him, anyone who teaches Feng Shui without having a good foundation in classical Chinese thought is like someone practising surgery without first studying anatomy. He feels that knowledge of the fundamental concepts is necessary so that individuals who have not studied China may have a better appreciation of such a venerable art and science.

According to him, a Neolithic grave unearthed not so long ago in the Henan province is a microcosm of the Chinese world as it was perceived in this early period. Its southern face (beyond the head of the skeleton) was round, while the northern face (at the skeleton's foot) was square.

This accords with later images of the cosmos wherein the earth was represented by the square body of a chariot and heaven by its round, umbrella-like canopy. More importantly, the remains of the body were accompanied by two figures outlined in shells, a dragon to the east and a tiger to the west. In the centre of the grave was a representation of Bei Dou, the Northern Ladle (or Dipper). Since the dragon and tiger are also constellations in the Chinese sky, it is clear that the Yangshao people were already orienting their tombs with the annual revolution of the Big Dipper around the North Star.

Qi (popularly spelt *chi*) rides the feng (wind) and scatters, but is retained when encountering shui (water). The ancients collected it to prevent its dissipation and guided it to assure its retention. Thus it was called Feng Shui.

As per the laws of Feng Shui, the site that attracts water is optimum, followed by the site that catches the wind. In its earliest form, Feng Shui was utilised to orient the homes of the dead rather than the homes of the living. The term itself appears first in a passage from the *Book of Burial*, which dates to no earlier than the fourth century BCE.

Understanding the Concept

Explaining the concept of *qi*, Dr Field says that thousands of pages of commentary have been dedicated to the explanation of this term and, quite frankly, no English translation can do it justice. While 'energy' may capture some of its physical characteristics, such a word does not address its metaphysical qualities. The *Book of Burial* characterises it as 'life breath'. In India, however, we refer to the same energy as *prana*.

In one of its earliest contexts (*The Zuo Commentary*, 541 BCE), *qi* is a meteorological category composed of the six phases of cold, warmth, wind, rain, darkness, and light. While it originally meant steam or vapour (as in clouds), by the time of Confucius it had come to mean an animating force in the atmosphere (manifested in weather phenomena) that actively influenced the human body (manifested in fever, chills, delusions, etc).

The science of Feng Shui analysed this force in the environment with the intention of controlling its manifestations in the individual. Such analysis was scientific only insofar as it was based on empirical observation. When other factors such as numerology and astrology were consulted, Feng Shui became less a science and more an art.

The science of Feng Shui in its earliest recorded context specifically refers to the School of Forms. Terrestrial features serve to block the wind – which captures qi and scatters it, and channel the waters – which collect qi and store it. Feng Shui may literally indicate "wind and water", but this is merely shorthand for an environmental policy of "hindering the wind and hoarding the waters". The science of Feng Shui, therefore, is "windbreak-watercourse qimancy".

Dr Field continues, "The art of *Kanyu* [Feng Shui], on the other hand, the precursor of the Compass School, relies strictly on astrology and numerology as a means of fathoming qi on a cosmic scale. While Feng Shui is local, Kanyu is universal. Since the medieval period in China – the existence of competing schools notwithstanding – masters of Qimancy were versed in the environmental science as well as the occult art. The term I have coined, Qimancy, divination according to qi, applies to both."

Dwelling on the origins further, Dr Field points out that China, like its sister civilisations in Greece and India, developed a very sophisticated science of astronomy in its pre-classical period. Both solar and lunar eclipses are recorded on oracle bones from the mid-fourteenth to the mid-thirteenth centuries BCE. The most ancient extant record of a nova, or stellar explosion, is also contained in an oracle bone dating to circa 1300 BCE.

The sighting of Halley's Comet was first recorded by Chinese astronomers in the classical period (467 BCE).

And sunspots were observed without the aid of telescopes as early as 28 BCE. (Myths of sun ravens may be earlier references to this solar phenomenon.) While the Chinese did not have telescopes, they did invent other scientific instruments.

Rising Popularity

Feng Shui is rapidly becoming a standard practice for creating the ideal environment in which to live and work. This ancient Chinese study of the natural and "built" environment has been practised for thousands of years. This environment can be at the office, in your home, in a building, or on real property. A Feng Shui analysis examines the surrounding environment, the building, how the people interact with the building and looks at time-related factors. Based upon these considerations, recommendations can be made on how to improve your relationship with the environment around you. Results include prosperity, health benefits, and well-being.

Properly applied, Feng Shui recommendations can result in improvements in the life of the individuals who occupy the property.

Feng Shui can be termed a form of 'geomancy' or 'earth wisdom'. Many cultures in the world have a form of geomancy in their history. The Chinese form of geomancy, or Feng Shui, has evolved to be both a science and an art. The science comes from the calculations and methodology used in analysing a property.

The art of Feng Shui is the wisdom acquired from performing a multitude of analysis and knowing the exact degree to which the remedies (which are the results of the scientific analysis) are prescribed. Throughout ancient China, classical Feng Shui was a closely guarded discipline used as a tool to ensure the good health, wealth, and power of the imperial dynasties.

The keepers of this secret body of knowledge – the Feng Shui masters – were highly respected meteorologists, astronomers, and other scientists who were charged with sustaining the good fortune and prosperity of the royal court. It has been guardedly passed down the generations through very specific lineages. These masters were very selective of their protégées. Extreme care was exercised in the selection of candidates who would become their successors.

ooo

Understanding the Basics

Feng Shui is based on the principle of Yin and Yang. Balance, harmony, consistent change, and the interdependency of all things are but a few of the deep meanings within this simple representation. Yang representing heat and light rises and Yin representing cold and darkness descends. These are just two of the many examples of logic and insight to be discovered within this image.

Yang, representing heat, rises on the left (or east) and reaches its peak at the top (south). Yin, representing coolness, descends on the right (west) and reaches its maximum at the bottom (north). Another analogy is that the sun rises in the east, reaches its hottest at noon and sets in the west, soon reaching its darkest. Yet within Yin there is a seed of Yang waiting to rise and within

Yang there is Yin waiting to descend. This analogy can be applied to time, seasons, directions, and many other cycles of change.

The Relationship of Five Elements

Another simple, yet powerful representation based upon the *Tai Chi* (Yin and Yang representation) is the five elements diagram. It is a view of how the elemental energies interact. In its balanced state, it is in harmony. Yet each element can strengthen or weaken other elements in a variety of beneficial and detrimental ways. When calculating the energy 'blueprint' of a property these interactions provide the key to correcting issues within a property.

The Eight Trigrams

The Eight Trigrams are the basis for Feng Shui analysis and calculations. A trigram is a representation of one of the eight directions.

In the *Ba Gua* there is a centre that has no directional association, but is associated with earth. Based also on Yin and Yang concepts, the *I Ching*, the *Five Elements*, and the *Lo-shu* map, it conveys a map for all other calculations used to determine the energy blueprint within a property.

Both people and houses belong to one of the trigrams. Each of the trigrams falls into two distinct categories as either east group or west group. Matching a west group house type to a west group person is ideal, as is matching an east group house to an east group person. There are advanced techniques too, which use the Eight Trigrams with particular calculations to derive the specific nature of the building and create its energy blueprint. They are too extensive and inhabit the inner reaches of the purist's theories.

Explaining the concept in depth may be outside the ambit of this book, as this is only a primer and not an encyclopaedia on Feng Shui. We have, anyway, roped in a lot of ancient China and dwelt on its ethos to provide the reader with an authentic background of Feng Shui. So much of Feng Shui is bandied about these days with little or no explanation of its origins.

Applying the Principles

Feng Shui is based upon a set of theories and complex calculations derived from the *I Ching*. This includes an in-depth understanding and application of the basic principles. Using these principles and taking into account the physical relationship between the natural environment and the magnetic fields of the earth provides a 'blueprint' of the influences around us. Using this blueprint, practitioners can clearly see the energies or *chi* that affect us in our properties.

Feng Shui Analysis

The Feng Shui practitioner first observes the environment, using a *Lo Pan* (compass) to determine the orientation of the property. Calculations are then completed according to the basic principles. Then a determination of the energy characteristics within the property and its resulting effects on the occupants is made based on the results of these calculations. Remedies are then prescribed where necessary in order to balance the energy to produce a positive effect.

Feng Shui is now becoming more prevalent in the West. This can be attributed to more and more people becoming aware of how their environment affects them. The health effects of high-tension power lines are but one example of how people are becoming aware of their environment and its relationship to their health and prosperity. Unfortunately, a lot of hearsay and misunderstandings as to what Feng Shui truly is has also become commonplace.

Some people have confused Feng Shui with religion and burning charms. Others think that seeking advice from Feng Shui practitioners contradicts the doctrines of their own religion. This is a mistaken concept.

Chinese geomancy (or Feng Shui) is not the product of any religious belief system. Rather, it is based on a set of calculations. The qualified practitioner examines the four aspects of Building, Environment, Time, and most importantly, People.

Most books and information widely available only look at the first two aspects: Building and Environment. This is only a partial examination. Time and People are two very important components that should not be omitted. A particular building may have a good environment and other positive attributes, but for a specific individual, it might require further examination and corrections to meet his individual goals for that time in his life and the life of the building.

Finding a Qualified Practitioner

The classical Feng Shui consultation involves no guesswork. Every building has unique energy characteristics that need to be individually addressed. We say that true Feng Shui recommendations utilise only the five elements and not such things as mirrors, flutes, incense, or prayers. Just as a qualified physician will not make a prescription without first meeting the patient, a proper Feng Shui analysis requires a visit to the property. Feng Shui looks at not only the environment, but also the orientation of the property within that environment. Feng Shui is not related to any religion or belief system.

A qualified practitioner is one who has studied with a master for many years and has acquired a scientific discipline, thus enabling him to apply complex calculations and an in-depth understanding of the fundamental principles of Feng Shui. Only then will s/he be able to make very specific recommendations that can effect positive changes in one's lifestyle, relationships and financial returns.

Properly performed, Feng Shui can bring balance, harmony and prosperity to one's life.

Finding Your Own Trigram and Directions

To find out how best to position yourself at home and at work, find your trigram based on your birth date and then determine your favourable and unfavourable directions. Feng Shui is based on the solar calendar, not the lunar calendar. The commonly known 'Chinese New Year' is typically the lunar calendar. Some forms of Chinese astrology are based on the lunar calendar, but Feng Shui is based on the sun, which influences our seasons and dictates our climates.

The Chinese hold February 4 as the 'Spring Establishment', or the time when the new solar year begins. If you were born before February 4, you belong to the prior year's trigram. If you were born on February 4 or 5, you should check with Feng Shui advisors for the exact trigram based on the time of your birth.

All this may appear a little complicated and so a good Feng Shui advisor is essential. The study of Feng Shui is like an onion. You can peel away the layers one by one and discover that there are other influences or levels. Feng Shui is truly a lifelong study.

The Importance of a Compass

Feng Shui is only Feng Shui if a compass is used. Without it, one is only practising design and personal preference. A Feng Shui analysis is very specific. Let's see how specific it is. There are eight directions: North, South, East, West, North-east, South-east, North-west, and North-east. On a *Lo Pan*, or Chinese compass, these directions are divided into three different sections. On a *Lo Pan* then, there are 24 divisions of 15 degrees each. Each division's orientation can result in a totally different house in terms of its prosperity. A few degrees one way or another is a completely different house type.

One of the most important aspects of Feng Shui is time. To find out just how important the time factor is, the purists multiply the 24 divisions by the nine different time periods (a time period here is 20 years) and so we can see that there are really 216 different house types, not just 24. Multiply this with an unlimited number of floor plans and you get an infinite number of Feng Shui analyses.

One size does not fit all. There is no fixed area for wealth, health, etc. These forms of *qi* can be present, but it takes a qualified practitioner to uncover them. Further, there are variable *qi* energies depending on the time. These are 180 years, 20 years, annually, monthly, and daily.

So what does all this mean? Well, if you are in a house that was built between 1964 and 1983, then in 1984 it became weaker. And during this 20-year period, there is the possibility that a house can be 'restricted' or have difficult periods for either the people or money. This lasts for the particular time cycle. It can be a month, year, or even 20 years. This explains why a lot of times that a particular house can be very good, but for a certain year, money is a struggle, or perhaps relationships are difficult to find. All of this is based on calculations. Feng Shui can be very exact. It is not guesswork. What makes it confusing is that there are practitioners with varying degrees of knowledge.

There are many different levels of Chinese Feng Shui. The commonly used teachings include: *Form* – the *Form* Method addresses only the external or internal environments. *Eight House* – (also known as the East/West teachings) this method addresses the basic orientations and how best to align oneself to the favourable directions. *Xuan Kong* – (also known as Flying Star Method) this is a time-specific Feng Shui, which looks at orientations and time factors. This is used to map the specific *qi* within a building, room, or other area. This is a very detailed method and can be very accurate if performed correctly. These methods are all necessary and work together. You can analyse the Feng Shui on a *Form* level without a compass, but you are only dealing with such issues as 'clearing the clutter' or how the outside environment affects the house.

The *Eight House* theory is based on orientation and requires a compass. If you use *Xuan Kong*, which deals with specific issues of *chi*, then you also must look at *Form* as well as the *Eight House* theories to accurately analyse the Feng Shui. With this method, you must have an accurate compass reading. To look at Feng Shui any deeper than the *Form* Method, you must use a compass to determine the direction. Many times, people think their house faces a certain direction, but are incorrect when a compass is used.

Many cities are based on grids that are North/South or East/West. But is it true North or magnetic North? Feng Shui looks at magnetic North. So remember, if there is no exact measurement of orientation, then there is no way to judge the Feng Shui beyond the basic environment. A complete Feng Shui analysis uses all three methods to accurately look at the environment of the building and how the people can feel their best in that building.

Time Aspect of Feng Shui

Time marches on. It waits for no man. It is ephemeral and elusive. Time controls our lives. People live by their calendars and their watches. It is also a principal part of Feng Shui, which is based on change. Change occurs with time.

There is a lot of talk about Feng Shui these days. Most books and practitioners address Feng Shui in a static manner. Feng Shui, however, is not static. It is constantly undergoing change. It is based on the *I Ching* or *Book of Change*. This Chinese oracle tells us that everything undergoes change. Feng Shui is a process of mapping these changes within an environment.

Timing and Mapping of the Earth

Time cycles in different measurements. According to the Chinese masters, Feng Shui cycles in multi-year increments, annual increments, and even monthly and daily cycles.

Feng Shui was an observational science more than 2,500 years ago and as such, the ancients observed the earth, as well as the heavens. They observed the cycles of the planets, constellations, seasons, and life. By drawing a co-relation between the seasons and astronomical movements, these early masters realised that there was a timing to when earthly events happened. They mapped out a solar year that correlates to the 'Spring Establishment' or the Chinese beginning of spring. This usually occurs on February 4 or 5. This timing was chosen as it is halfway between the winter solstice and the spring equinox. Just as wood starts the beginning of the cycle of the five elements, the spring establishment is the start of the new annual cycle.

Further mapping the timing of the earth, an evolved Feng Shui study began. This study is known as *Xuan Kong*. This study began to look at how timing affects buildings, people, and their environment. Working with their knowledge of directional Feng Shui, the early masters found a system that allowed them to assess why certain events happened in certain areas of a house during a certain time.

Over 2,500 years, *Xuan Kong* has evolved and now it is highly accurate in mapping the timing of events associated with the movement of *chi*. Just as the orbits of the planets can be calculated, so can the *chi* energy within a building. While it is a complex system, it follows the same methods and calculations again and again. It has even been programmed into the computer. Using such a programme will give you a print-out of results, but it does not give you a complete Feng Shui analysis. It takes a trained master to synthesise these calculations with the environment, the architecture, and the people who occupy these environments.

Chi itself cycles with time. There are 180-year cycles, 60-year cycles, 20-year cycles, and annual cycles. It is stronger in new buildings and weakens over time. On a practical or environmental level, farmers have to rotate their crops to avoid exhausting the ground. The ground loses its nutrients over time. Some years later, the same area of the earth can be used again.

Similarly, *chi* of a house tires after some time. The *chi* gets gradually weaker until it cycles around, gets its 'second wind', and becomes strong again. This happens over a long period of time.

Consider a 180-year-old house. Chances are, it is now remodelled and is thought of as a classic. It has a freshness about it that a house of 80 years does not have. The most vibrant, though, is a brand new building. It has the strongest *chi* energy. Even so, if it was an ideal Feng Shui house when first built, it will remain a good house throughout its life. Similarly, if it was an undesirable Feng Shui house when it was first built, it will remain undesirable throughout its life.

Even cities have this cycle of vitality. New developments are strong and vibrant, but after 40 or more years, they decline. Buildings built in the 1950s do not have the same vitality that a modern 2000s building has. Areas of the city that were built 60 years ago are not as vibrant as areas that are brand new.

Think about cities in Asia that are currently flourishing. In Hong Kong, for example, new buildings are replacing old ones all the time. The residents there understand that, properly applied, Feng Shui of a new building is better than an older building. This is true with many Chinese cities as well. Cities that are rebuilding themselves are cities that will be prosperous, especially if proper Feng Shui principles are applied.

Currently we are in a *Tui* time cycle (1984-2003). *Tui* is the trigram that is represented by the number 7. It also relates to the mouth or communication. It is also a very social and sometimes frivolous time. During this time, communication is strong. This timing has coincided with the emergence of the Internet. This time period is good for people (including national leaders) who use their mouth for a living. Attorneys, entertainers, and singers are in their prime time period.

The last time period was *Chien* (1964-1984). This was a time of strong leaders. *Chien* is usually associated with strong, hard metal. It was a time of extremes. The next time period is *Ken* (2004-2023). This time is a time for youth and simplicity. We should see younger leaders and life should be not as complicated as it is now.

ooo

Mystical Belief or Natural Science?

Just as the earth is constantly moving and changing, so are the energies of Feng Shui. Modern science has shown that geomagnetics are in a constant flux. Feng Shui calculations show changing results based on the variables of building, people, time, and environment. There is no fixed place for money, love, or study. Although the *chi* for these objectives exists, they are found in different places in different buildings. It takes a qualified practitioner who knows how to uncover these locations.

Much has been said about the 'cures' used in Feng Shui. But traditional Feng Shui does not prescribe any flutes, mirrors, charms, chants, or other mystical objects. Rather, a qualified practitioner only utilises the five Chinese elements of wood, fire, earth, metal and water to bring a place into an energetic balance. These elements can take the form of many objects such as a brass pot, or an aquarium, but the actual remedies are still strictly the element.

Many books have written about using mirrors as a Feng Shui cure. In actuality, mirrors used to be made of polished brass (a metal remedy) and in the Middle Ages it worked as a cure. Modern mirrors do not have enough of the metal element to be prescribed as a remedy. Today, when asked about where to put the mirror, most qualified practitioners answer: "In the bathroom, which is where it is needed most!" Although a mirror can be used architecturally to hide a pillar or make the room appear larger, it is not a Feng Shui remedy.

The objective of the remedies is to return a natural balance of *chi* (or life energy) to a building. Feng Shui remedies are only based on the natural elements and not the objects themselves. As for avoidance of sharp angles, just as in art, rounded edges are much more beautiful and pleasing than angles. This is part of the environmental aspect of Feng Shui.

There are a lot of benefits to having a proper Feng Shui analysis performed. People have reported increases in wealth and love, and significant improvements in health. Feng Shui can be shown to be both a science and an art. The science of Feng Shui is the detailed analysis of the four aspects using mathematical calculations. The art of Feng Shui is the experience of how to best implement the remedies. How much, exactly where, and for how long, are the skills of a practised Feng Shui master.

Feng Shui is not about making drastic changes, but making energetic improvements in your living space that will result in the best possible benefits for all who reside there. Today unfortunately, there is much hearsay, superstition and nonsense about Feng Shui. On the contrary, the origins and early applications of Feng Shui as per the dictates of the purists makes complete sense and is based on logic and scientific principles.

The Fish Factor

This is a Feng Shui topic that creates a lot of confusion, primarily because there is some basis for what is discussed, but there is also a lot of misunderstanding. In traditional Chinese Feng Shui, the only recommended solutions are the five elements of wood, fire, earth, metal, and water. The water element strengthens wood *chi*. Fish have been confused to be a Feng Shui remedy, but this is not true.

In Feng Shui, the numbers 6 and 7 are used in the calculations of the trigrams and are representative of metal (6 = *Chien* or hard metal, and 7 = *Tui* or soft metal). The

Five Elements theory says that metal strengthens water. Chinese folklore says that adding 6 gold fish and one black fish makes the water stronger. What this is trying to do is to strengthen the water effect with metal. Actually, the fish only add decoration to the tank. To really strengthen the water element, the tank should have the real metal element with the water.

Fish do add a couple of things though. One is beauty and the other is to add circulation to the water. Further, they are living creatures and they bring life to the environment. This is good Feng Shui, but it is not needed in a strict sense for the water element to be effective. The water element will work with or without the fish, as long as it is kept clean and circulating. Avoid stagnant water. This becomes a *sha* (negative influence) and is not helpful.

Why Feng Shui?

In recent times, Feng Shui has experienced a tremendous growth in the western world. Internet Usenet, websites, books, television and other forms of media contain an ambient buzz about Feng Shui. So why is there this resurgence in popularity of an ancient science? What do people hope Feng Shui will accomplish in their lives?

Feng Shui is about balance, comfort and harmony. Feng Shui is not a religion or a mystical belief. Rather, it is a science that offers the ability to create a balance in your dwelling or place of work. It is no coincidence that with the end of this millennium, we are in a *Tui* cycle of Feng Shui. *Tui* is the trigram that is associated with entertainment and communication. Despite hurdles, the movie industry is booming and the Internet is leading to communication never before seen in the world. Its resurgence in popularity might be attributed to this time period, but the science of Feng Shui remains squarely rooted in architecture, astronomy, physics, and design.

Feng Shui uses observation, repeatable calculations and methodologies, and is based on the study of the environment around, both inside and outside. *Kan Yu*, the original name for Feng Shui, literally translates into "Raise the head and observe the sky above. Lower the head and observe the environment around us."

Feng Shui in Business

A small example may help illustrate a point. For years, a property management company had a beautiful metal statue in their conference room, which attracted a lot of attention as well as compliments. But, during a rearrangement of the office, they moved the statue to an area outside the conference room. About six months later, in a Feng Shui consultation, it was suggested that they needed the metal element inside the conference room to avoid money delays.

When told this, the principals of the company were astonished. They thought back over the period without the statue in the conference room and realised that money and clients were hard to come by. They quickly moved it back in, and the old windfall returned. While metal is not always the correct solution, it was required in this case to minimise delays and create a warm and inviting area to greet clients.

Feng Shui, properly applied, can greatly contribute to the growth of a business. In one company, three offices were recommended as being ideal for storage, but harmful if used for offices. Not surprisingly, it was revealed to the Feng Shui practitioner that these offices consistently remained empty and the staff who had occupied them previously, had either quickly left the company after a short tenure or had developed serious illnesses. The hidden costs to a company of having undiscovered 'critical' areas include leaves of absence and increased sick time at work.

When utilising space planning or considering an expansion, Feng Shui should be taken into account to minimise the negative effects of certain areas and to enhance other, more productive areas. Especially important are the entrances to the building and offices, the executive offices, the sales and marketing areas, and the conference rooms where important decisions and negotiations occur. Promoting good *chi* in these areas can have a strong impact on prosperity. Using Feng Shui principles in laying out office space, one can avoid common mistakes that lead to sales declines, unhappy employees and low turnover.

Some basic Feng Shui advice that business owners need be aware of is: Provide direct views to an entrance; don't place an employee with his back to the entrance of an office or cubicle; and avoid placing an employee in the direct line of a door because it erodes privacy and can create a feeling of always being watched. Additionally, it sets the employee directly in the rush of *chi* and can have negative effects on health and productivity.

Lastly, utilise warm lighting (as opposed to glarish florescent lighting), if possible. Lighting can change the entire atmosphere of a room and so keep it balanced, neither too bright nor too low. It is in the realms of common sense and Feng Shui to maintain a pleasing environment for higher productivity.

In addition to the environment, the balance of *chi* (life energy) needs to be considered. *Chi* is specific to a building and orientation. A good example of this is when a successful restaurant moves and then goes out of business within a few months. Identifying a good Feng Shui location should be taken into account when relocating your business. A qualified practitioner can analyse the environment both inside and outside and determine the orientation of the building. Using time-proven calculations, the practitioner can make recommendations on whether the building would be supportive and if it is, how best to balance the *chi*.

When creating balanced *chi*, traditional Feng Shui utilises only the five natural elements of wood, fire, earth, metal, and water to create balanced environments. Feng Shui can be fine-tuned to the staff members. Key employees can be positioned in such a way that they are oriented to their most productive direction. Each person has an association with one of the eight directions. These directions can be either positive or less than favourable depending upon the individual. A qualified practitioner should be used to determine the advantageous direction for each person.

While strategy, keen business sense, strong goals, excellent management and a good deal of common sense can move a company forward, more and more businesses are utilising Feng Shui to ensure that there are no roadblocks to creating the success that the company desires. A productive and harmonious environment can only support the employees and generate additional revenues from clients who, for reasons not readily apparent to them, enjoy returning to such a warm place of business.

Feng Shui is a study of the environment; specifically the living spaces we call home or work. When we are at home, we need a restful environment. Many times though, homes are designed and built in a shape that is not conducive to rest. Rather, it stirs you up or is unsettling. A well-designed house should allow the owner to enjoy a comfortable experience within the house. Often in an effort to make a statement or to add a personal uniqueness, especially these days with a lot of money and ideas floating around, architects play with the shape of a house. These unique designs and floor plans can have a significant effect on the people who occupy the home.

In Feng Shui, shapes can have a profound effect on the Feng Shui within a home or building, in the process helping or impairing the occupants and their well-being. To provide some oft-quoted examples: One such case was a house where people entered at a right 45-degree turn. Without fail, everyone who entered that house tripped over his or her own feet. Another house was designed in a half circle. The house had circular walls and had almost triangular rooms. The owner of this home suffered from health and relationship problems.

The reason many Chinese restaurants use circular tables rather than square ones is that circles create unstable *chi* that is constantly circulating. Square tables create restful *chi*. People tend to linger longer at a square table. The same goes for a circular house. The *chi* is not still. It does not create a restful home. People do not tend to stay long in a circular home. Triangular-shaped houses and lots are not preferred either. There is an imbalance in this shape. One side is open and the other very close. Inside the house, odd angles are created in the rooms.

In Feng Shui, odd angles are not preferred, especially those that point at you. They direct the *chi* at you. Often this is called 'poison arrows'. Also called *sha chi*, this is simply a flow of *chi* that is too strong. Just like sleeping directly under a ventilator, and awaking with a cramp, *sha chi* can affect your well-being. Triangular rooms, homes, or lots can create a lot of these *sha chi*.

Alternatively, a square or rectangular house is ideal. These are stable and solid. People naturally feel at home. The *chi* can settle in a square room. The floor plan for a square or rectangular house is usually logical and easy to navigate. Whereas the floor plan of a triangular house is often confusing with 45-degree turns and oddly placed doors.

While the home shape is important, the lot that the building sits on is also very significant. Triangular lots can restrict either the well-being of the people or the financial success of the home. This is another area where a square or rectangular shape is very important. If the lot has a triangular shape, use bushes or a treeline to square off the lot.

When looking for a home or even selecting an office, try to find the home that is square, or rectangle and allows you to walk through it without getting confused. If you have a home with angles, try to block those angles using nice plants that cover the angle and block the *sha chi*. If you have a circular house, you can also use the plants to slow down the *chi* and to create lines within that feel more natural. You can check this out yourself. It is not the mumbo-jumbo of some esoteric science. There is a lot of common sense in all this.

The next time you find yourself in an unusually shaped building, stop and notice the feeling you get from the building's design. Are you confused? Do you know where to go? Do you feel dizzy? Notice your environment and its effects on you. This is Feng Shui!

Buildings designed with Feng Shui in mind, while perhaps architecturally plain, can promote one's success and well-being. The idea simply is to allow the space to energise you.

ooo

The Question of Consultation

There are innumerable questions about Feng Shui consultations. The most common is "What does a consultation consist of?" Most people have never experienced a Feng Shui consultation or have only heard about it. What should one expect? How soon does one see results? What is a fair rate? Is there much truth to it? Is it expensive? Will it mean a complete restructuring? ...And so on. There are so many questions and so many different answers depending on whom you ask.

We will try to answer these questions and clear up some of the mystery of what is involved with a traditional Feng Shui consultation. If we go back in history to one of the very first Feng Shui masters, Yang Yun-Sung, also known as 'Yang save the poor', we learn that Feng Shui was based on creating a balance. Following the concept of Yin and Yang, Master Yang tried to balance his work. After having served the imperial leaders in the palace, he began to assist the common people. His goal was to help people. This is and should be the foremost goal of any good Feng Shui practitioner.

In fact, when analysing a house the goal is to help the people first and the pecuniary aspects should come later. If the people are in ill health or have relationship problems, the money is not the criterion at all. So a Feng Shui practitioner must be one who sincerely wants to help.

When providing a consultation, a qualified practitioner should take four things into account: the building, the environment, the time, and the people. Most books, websites, and other literature on the subject speak about the building and environment. Actually, the people and timing are equally important for an accurate analysis. A house that is good for one person may not be good for another and this year might bring some beneficial or unfavourable situations for one family, which may be wholly untrue in the case of another family inhabiting the same space.

Feng Shui believes that everything is undergoing change. Nothing is fixed. Time is consistently changing. *Qi* or *chi* is continually changing. So each house during different time periods is different as the energy flow is different.

Find a practitioner who understands this concept and who is aware that individuals play an important part in the analysis. Before the consultation begins, a qualified practitioner should be given the following details: The birth dates of the occupants. The date the building was built. A proportional floor plan and an appointment to actually see the building…

The birth dates determine the trigram of the people and help find their best directions. The date the building was built is used in the calculations to determine the *chi* within the building. The floor plan is used to properly map the *chi*. And the appointment is needed because even with photographs and accurate descriptions, there is no substitute for actually experiencing the home or building firsthand.

The actual consultation can be anywhere from one to four hours or more depending on the complexity of the building. Typically, the first thing to be examined, before anything else, is the exterior environment. The Feng Shui practitioner is looking for any *sha* or negative influence. Things such as overgrown trees that create too Yin an environment, the noise *sha* from living too close to a busy road, to construction going on nearby, among other types of pollutants, are distractions that can create concern. Don't worry though if you have these things in your environment. While they are not favourable, there are many variations of these situations and most are easily correctable. Trimming the trees or putting up new trees to buffer the noise from the road are examples of easy remedial measures.

The next step in a consultation is to examine the interior environment. Again, before any actual 'analysis' is done, the Feng Shui master should understand the situation. A real master should be able to tell you some of the issues that might be going on based on their careful analysis. You could also brief him about your specific area of trouble. It is almost like a doctor's consultation. The more you reveal, the more accurate the diagnosis.

A good practitioner should be able to determine the usual and common money and health problems from his calculations. But there are other aspects of diagnosis too. For example: a person who belongs to the *Chen* Trigram (wood) might have problems with the throat sleeping in an area that predominantly consists of metal *chi*. Metal dominates wood. *Chen* relates to the throat. Once the environmental assessment is done, the master will find the orientation using a *Lo Pan* or Chinese compass.

This will help in determining the exact orientation of the house. A few degrees of variation can make the difference between a good house and an unfavourable house. Feng Shui is about making things better. So even if you might live in an unfavourable house, there are remedies that can be applied that will create the balance to even things out. After the orientation is determined, the master will perform the calculations to determine what needs to be balanced.

In early China, the masters wore robes with large sleeves. They would put their hands together inside the sleeves. Unnoticed, they used the first three fingers on their hand to perform the calculations. If you count the pads on the three fingers, you will find that there are nine pads arranged in roughly the same grid as a trigram. Today, of course, there are computers and other sophistry.

The last step is to sit down with the client and discuss the findings.

The remedies suggested should fit nicely into your environment and consist only of introducing one of the five elements into your building or home and perhaps some suggestions on how to make the environment more pleasing. Subtlety is the key. If your house looks like it has been Feng Shui'd, then it wasn't the best application of Feng Shui remedies. Feng Shui remedies should not be apparent. It should look natural and beautiful. Not forced or uncomfortable.

After applying the suggested remedies, the million-dollar question arises – when should one expect results? Typically, results can occur within a month. Keep in mind that many times they are so subtle and gradual you might not notice them. Other times, it is a few days later that something amazing happens. Do not expect amazing results though. Many times, Feng Shui does not change the apparent, but rather creates a space that will allow doors to open. If there are health issues, do not expect to be cured immediately. But the process of positive change will have begun.

Feng Shui creates the environment that is supportive for recovery. An example: one client was in an unfavourable house and knew it. He asked if he should sell his house. The answer given was to apply the remedies and see what happens. In about a month, he received a job offer that he couldn't refuse and ended up moving as a necessity of the new job!

When people ask how much a consultation should cost, the answer is difficult. The best answer is to invest what is comfortable for you for a Feng Shui consultation and reasonable for the size of the project. Of course, nowadays with the fashion statement that Feng Shui has become, charges can be high. But when providing a consultation, there needs to be value in it for the client. When they see things working, they also get encouraged to go the whole way.

Today, Feng Shui practitioners are newspaper columnists and earn a lot of fame. Some of them are certainly good but, like in every other profession, there are also many who have wormed into positions of eminence. It is essential to sift the chaff from the grain.

Ask questions, search for reasonable answers and build a comfort level with the practitioner. Feng Shui is about comfort and harmony. You don't have to do anything that does not sound right or does not make sense to you. Find a practitioner you are comfortable with and keep asking questions till you are satisfied with his knowledge. You don't have to accept somebody and pay him a colossal fee just because his face appears in your favourite newspaper every week.

Read between the lines. Don't fall for the esoteric and what you can't understand. Ask for simple explanations. It's your space, your money and your life. It's your right to know.

ooo

Landscaping and the Elements

Feng Shui is the study of the 'built' environment. While it does look at the larger environment surrounding the structure, there are no hard and fast rules about the landscaping. Feng Shui is primarily focused on the *chi* within a structure, as that is what has the most direct effect on the people. When it comes to the outside environment, the main point of concern is that the landscaping should be beautiful and in balance with the rest of the environment. Living in a beautiful environment is much more supportive than living in an environment that is an eyesore. You can tell the *chi* of a neighbourhood or area by how green and glossy the trees and plants are.

Some general rules: Pathways should flow like a meandering stream and not a straight road. Trees are most welcome but they should not be placed in a direct line with any entrances, especially the main entrance. Try to keep a balance of Yin and Yang (dark and light) when thinking of the trees. Avoid trees that will completely block the light. Too much of anything is not good. Again, balance is the key. Shrubbery is okay as long as it is kept neat and prevented from overgrowing.

Trees and shrubbery can be used to block harsh *chi* such as strong winds. Grass does not pose any problems. Strive for beauty. Flowers and other colourful plants can be used as long as they fit within the environment and follow the rules of the five elements. Wood produces fire, fire produces earth, earth produces metal, metal produces water, and water produces wood. Wood is green, fire is red, earth is tans or yellow, metal is white or gold, and water is blue or black. Avoid using them in a destructive combination such that "wood uproots earth, earth blocks water, water douses fire, fire melts metal, and metal chops wood".

Consider the direction the building 'sits'. For example, if the building faces the north and sits to the south, then this is a *Li* building (*Li* is the fire trigram). This house would be supported by a lot of red flowers, but would not benefit from blue or black colours. A house that sits to the west and faces east is a *Tui* structure (*Tui* is a soft metal trigram) and would benefit from white and gold flowers. Reds and purples should be avoided. This can also apply to the colour of the house trim as well. These are all general rules and while their effect can be minimal on the house itself, following the rules of balance can support the house and its occupants.

The two items that need to be looked at carefully are rocks and water. Since they are both part of the five elements and are used to remedy certain situations in the greater environment, they need to be placed very carefully. Water in the west is not good, while in the south-west and east it can assist prosperity. These directions should not be in front of or behind the house or building. If they are, it takes a qualified practitioner to determine if the water will have a positive or negative effect. If you are striving for the effect of the water element, then it is better not to use an earthen container such as a fountain made of rocks, since earth blocks water in the cycle of the elements. Metallic containers work well as metal strengthens water.

Often, metal troughs have effectively been used with beautiful plants and flowers planted around it to blend in with the environment. Ponds and pools can be used under the guidance of a trained Feng Shui practitioner. The same can be said of rocks, especially large decorative rocks. Because these are used in certain situations to correct specific problems, they need to be placed under the guidance of a Feng Shui practitioner. Placed haphazardly, they could have an adverse effect on the prosperity of the building.

A qualified Feng Shui practitioner can determine if the placement of these elements is needed or not. Feng Shui folklore states that a building should have a mountain behind it to support it. By using rocks and earth, you can create this mountain. While this sounds good, this is not true in every case. Each building is unique and needs to be looked at on a case-by-case basis.

To summarise, plants and other 'wood' elements are fine anywhere as long as they do not block the *chi* of the building and are used in balance. Colours can be used to assist the home as long as they fall within the rules of the five elements. Water and rocks need to be placed under the advice of a trained practitioner to avoid adversely affecting the occupants or their prosperity. When placed correctly, they can have a very supportive effect on the building or house. The goal of Feng Shui is to create a comfortable and beautiful environment. Strive for this when landscaping too. But again, ask a qualified practitioner to unravel the complexities and, of course, do what you also instinctively feel is right.

The Five Elements

The Five Elements are synonymous with Feng Shui and quite popular too. These elements: Wood, Fire, Earth, Metal, and Water are the foundation theory for Feng Shui balance. There also seems to be some confusion about just what these elements really are and how they work. Actually, it is easy to understand the elements and their significance. Using them properly and in the correct proportion is what separates a master from a student.

The following is a brief description of each of these elements and how they might be applied.

Wood

We start with the wood element since it is the beginning of new life. Just as spring brings new plants and new life, wood is the originator of the five elemental cycle. Many people mistakenly use wood furniture as a Feng Shui solution. The problem with wood furniture is that it is lifeless.

To harness the *chi* of wood, it is essential you use live wood! A shrub or bushy plant is ideal since it emits live *chi* and is also an excellent method of retaining *chi*. Plants recycle the air we breathe and can provide a natural filter for the air. A common Feng Shui problem is the staircase that empties into a doorway. A bushy plant can retain some of that *chi*, when it is placed either on the landing, or more ideally, at the bottom of the staircase.

Remember that you want a live plant, so maintain it. A dead plant holds no *chi* and is actually a *sha* (unsightly or bad influence).

Wood can be represented by the colour green. We find that the colours are not nearly as effective, though, as the actual element. When it comes to the wood element, there is rarely an occasion when you need to substitute the colour for a living plant. Wood represents the directions of east and the *Chen* Trigram. It also represents the southeast and the Sun Trigram.

Fire

The fire element is the most Yang of the elements. It is the hot summer or a blast of heat. If it is hot, it is even better. A red night light or a table lamp with a red shade makes excellent fire remedies. Fire represents the south and the *Li* Trigram.

Earth

Earth is an interesting element despite the rather commonplace conception of dirt. Many times earth is recommended for a larger environmental solution. In this case large granite boulders, or a beautiful clay statue can be used. Terracotta pots filled with potting soil make a great earth remedy. Earth also represents the mountain. Earth tone colours can be used, but they are not nearly as effective as the actual element. Earth represents the north-east or the *Ken* Trigram. It also represents the south-west or the *Kun* Trigram.

Additionally, it represents the 'centre' of the Master Trigram. Energetically speaking, *Kun* Earth and the centre representation (also called a star) of '5' can have negative influences, whereas the *Ken* Trigram (north-east, also referred to as the mountain) can have a very prosperous influence.

Metal

The most common solution, metal can be found in all forms. Copper, silver, gold, and bronze are a few variations of the metal element. Using the metal element can take on all sorts of creative ideas. A cast silver deer is one idea. A bronze plate hung on the wall is another one. Even iron weightlifter plates can be utilised as a metal solution. This can be done by stacking a few, then placing a brass pot upside down on top and creating a pedestal for a small plant or perhaps a metal statue. The quantity of the element is definitely there! The key thing to remember is that Feng Shui is about creating a beautiful environment.

When utilising the metal element, ensure that it is rounded and pleasing, not sharp and pointed. Metal is the most commonly used remedy for the negative earth energies as mentioned above. Ideally, the goal is to introduce Feng Shui elemental solutions that are not identifiable as Feng Shui remedies. Feng Shui objects that are unsightly or easily identified as a 'Feng Shui cure' are not recommended. It should blend into the environment and be beautiful.

The colours of white, silver, or gold can be used. Metal represents the *Tui* Trigram in the west. *Tui* is a soft metal like gold. It is also the *Chien* Trigram in the north-west. *Chien* is a hard metal like steel.

Water

Water is what gives life. Without it, we would not exist. Our bodies are mostly water. In Feng Shui, water is a very useful element. Water, when needed, should be clear and flowing. Stagnant water can create more problems than it solves. A simple aquarium, or even a small 'metal' fountain can be used. Do not use ceramic or other earthen fountains. This is a common mistake.

The earth element blocks water and neutralises its positive effect. A metal trough, a fountain, or even a fishpond can act as an environmental solution. Water has always been synonymous with power. Water has been used as an elemental solution by the emperors in the form of moats and by placing their palaces near bodies of water. Most flourishing cities are either located near water or have large lakes or rivers nearby. Residences close to water bodies are always sold or bought at a premium.

Water can be represented by the colours blue or black. Water represents the *Kan* Trigram in the north.

While the elements and their uses have been detailed above, make sure that they are not used haphazardly. Ideally, a proper Feng Shui analysis should be performed by a qualified practitioner. Used incorrectly, the elements can cause harm to relationships, health, or prosperity.

ooo

The Significance of Yin and Yang

It isn't common knowledge that Feng Shui has two sides. Feng Shui corresponds to both Yin and Yang. Yang House Feng Shui is what most people understand to be Feng Shui. This is the analysis and remedy of a house for the living. Yin House Feng Shui is about selecting the best possible gravesite for the deceased.

But why do the deceased need to have a good home? In Chinese culture, people believe that a body inauspiciously buried can have an effect on the living for the next three generations. On the other hand, if you bury someone in the correct orientation, with the correct environment and at the right time, the family can prosper.

There are many examples of this: legend has it that Bruce Lee's father was buried inauspiciously. Therefore, both Bruce and Brandon suffered early deaths. This could hold true with the Kennedy family as well. It is also believed in China that the grave should be underground. Chiang Kai Shek, the former President of the Republic of China, was memorialised above the ground and it has been said that many tragedies affected the family.

Chinese culture is ancient and steeped in many labyrinths, nuances and layers of knowledge. Feng Shui was born in its embryo and so requires careful understanding. It is a complicated science and needs to be understood in its entirety with its historical perspective, the needs of the times, its functions, cures and priorities, which were more relevant at the time of its inception than it is today. Many things have, of course, changed, but the kernel of what once saved people, dynasties and the afterlife still holds good.

When a Feng Shui master looks to site a grave, he looks at the environment in detail. He looks at the mountains and the flow of the waterways. Commonly referred to as the Dragon, the mountains provide the support of the *chi* flow that a gravesite needs. But not all mountains are good. It takes a trained eye to differentiate the good and unfavourable mountains. The mountains should take the form of an armchair to support the grave.

The waterways are important as well, as they store the *chi*. Often referred to as the Dragon's veins, they flow down from mountain slopes, and how they flow is key to finding a good gravesite. Once the proper environment is chosen, the correct orientation for the body needs to be determined.

How you orient the body can affect different family members. Each of the trigrams has a family relationship.

One can find out who is affected based on the eight trigrams. Certain orientations can help the youngest members of the family while others can affect the elder members. The year in which the burial takes place is also important, just as in determining the year when a Yang house is built. When the body is buried, the energies for that time cycle are captured and will affect the descendants.

Lastly, the proper day selection is important. There should not be any conflict with the person's Chinese astrology. For example, a *Rat* person should not be buried on a *Horse* day and a *Rabbit* person should not be buried on a *Rooster* day. If you think all this is complicated, you haven't seen anything as yet. There are many other details. This is a simple example.

Feng Shui apprentices from hundreds of years ago used to follow their master for several years, walking the mountainsides and learning about the environment. They would then study with them for many more years to learn date selection and the calculations to determine the best *chi* energy. The key to remember is that not every Feng Shui person can properly site a grave, and if they do site a grave incorrectly, they are affecting three generations to come. This is serious karma to consider and so most practitioners of Yang House Feng Shui do not provide Yin House consultations.

All this is additional information and not strictly within the purview of the book. But a glimpse of Chinese ethos will help understand Feng Shui in a slightly more profound manner. When a race goes to great pains to orient the graves of the dead and when they consider the afterlife with such devotion and sanctity, one can then probably understand what goes into Feng Shui, into the practitioner, the consultation, and the way they look at all space. It is a sacred entity that needs to be energised from within and without.

The Practice

The application of object placement inside and outside the house is Feng Shui. Because it is rooted in *I Ching*'s binary language, Feng Shui is extremely technical. Although frequently criticised by students of Confucius, the application seeped into everyday life.

The palaces and tombs of the royal families built in the *Tang* dynasty (618-907) and all the following dynasties strictly followed the Feng Shui prescription. When Buddhism reached China, it soon absorbed the Feng Shui principles and combined it with its own practices. The historical Buddhist temples, most located at famous mountains in China, have all been built with Feng Shui in mind.

But the practice of Feng Shui was severely undermined in China in the twentieth century. With influences from the West seeping in beyond the awesome Great Wall, Chinese intellectuals began to question their heritage. Under the banner of 'learn from the West', Feng Shui began to be branded by many as mere 'superstition'. After 1949, the practice of Feng Shui was officially forbidden in the People's Republic of China. It was pitted along with other 'feudalistic superstitions'. While this was happening in the place of its birth, Feng Shui developed wings and spread all over the world.

Relevant Theories

To understand Feng Shui completely, we need to understand many theories on which it is based. Include *Yin-Yang, five elements, Ba-Gua, chi, ten heavenly stems* and *twelve earthly branches*. The ten heavenly stems are most frequently represented by using the *five elements* and Yin-Yang.

The *twelve earthly branches* are most well known as the twelve animals in the Chinese horoscope. The *twelve animals* are also related to the *five elements*. For example, the year 2000, which is the year of the dragon, has the character of earth. There is nothing good or bad about any element. The stockmarket can have a bear year in the Year of the Bull and the person born in the Year of the Pig can be really nice.

In Feng Shui, there are several schools that emphasise different aspects. There are a few basic dos and don'ts that are agreed upon by all practitioners and that form the crux of all consultation. Different schools have different interpretations and a person who wants to use it should pepper every theory with large doses of common sense.

Yin-Yang Philosophy

The most significant part of Chinese philosophy is the 'all-in-one' belief. The earth, the celestial objects and the human being are all one system. It is important to notice that in this one system there is no superior part or entity. Each and every part in the system has the ability to disturb it and cause it to deviate from the perfect harmony it strives to achieve. This 'lack of superiority' philosophy originated thanks to the pre-class society. Scarcity of food and other living material required every member of society to be extremely considerate to the other's needs. There was not even the co-existence of the Yin and Yang. It was simply a co-existence based on mutual support and survival because nobody could exist alone.

The growing awareness in the difference of the earth below and the celestial objects above, the men and women, the sun and the moon, the day and the night, started to appear much later on the philosophical level. The two sides are not as simple as the head and tail of a coin. It is much more profound.

It is even greater than an I-am-inside-you-while-you-are-inside-me type of co-existence. Yin is originated from Yang and Yang is originated from Yin. They encircle and embrace each other. Their constant moving balance is the ideal image of harmony.

Yin-Yang Symbol

Yin and Yang are the basic expressions of the ancient Chinese. It is equivalent to a *bit* in today's binary language. Each *Yao* (bit) represents either Yin (0), the female force of nature, or Yang (1), the male force of nature. Yin (0), female, is two short little hyphens with a gap in between. Yang, male, is one continuous hyphen-like line.

Certain historians believed that ancient man noticed the first difference between female (Yin) and male (Yang) from the most direct and important areas of our body. But it is important to know that the Chinese character for number one is exactly the same as the Yang (male) symbol, one continuous hyphen-like line.

Some historians would dispute it, but the ancient Chinese use the Yin (female) symbol to represent 'zero'. It is definitely appropriate and academically accepted to call it zero today. When the ancient symbols were first put into a computer, Yin (female) was represented by zero and one represented Yang (male).

Everything has Yin and Yang

It might not be difficult to understand that animals can be separated as Yin and Yang characters because they are female and male. That days are Yang and nights are Yin is easy to accept. We have no problem in agreeing that the Sun is Yang and the Moon is Yin. However, it must be emphasised that everything – the mountain, the plants and our body, all creatures the Lord made, everything that moves, breathes, lives – has Yin and Yang characters.

Everything has Yin and Yang, even within a Yin or Yang character. For example, the south of a mountain and the north of a river is Yang. What is the southern slope of a mountain that is also south of a river? It is on the Yang slope of the Yin riverside. Yin and Yang is rooted in the fact that the world is not homogeneous. There will always be conflicting or un-similar parts. Just like the northern and southern slopes of a mountain. The important part is to be able to identify the Yin and Yang characters in any given situation.

A few basic guidelines may help: Yin characters are even numbers, female, the moon, the earth, cold or cool feeling, night, darkness, soft, stable, closed, come (towards), down (directions), right (side), back, small, loyalty… to name a few. Nothing is fixed, but everything is ever changing.

Yang characters are odd numbers, male, the sun, the sky, hot or warm feeling, day, light, hard, moving, opened, go (away), up (direction), left (side), front, large, mercy. The co-existence of Yin and Yang is omnipresent. Their relationship needs to be understood.

Yin and Yang rely on each other. The Yin is defined as what is not Yang. Yang is defined as what is not Yin. Well, this might sound like one is chasing its own tail, but it is what the Yin-Yang philosophy is all about. Yin is inside Yang and Yang is inside Yin. Yin incubated and generated inside Yang. When Yin is extremely strong and elongated, it becomes Yang. The ultimate Yang character becomes Yin.

There is no permanent Yin or Yang. There is no absolute Yin or Yang. The Yin and Yang change is like the four seasons. The hottest summer days are the harbinger of winter. Yin and Yang are like day and night. The darkest moment of night is just before dawn. The Yin character becomes more evident when at the ultimate Yang. Yin exists in all types of Yang and vice versa.

Yin-Yang needs to mate. The need to mate is not merely sexual. It is the need for companionship and longing of one for the other. It motivates the movement towards each other. It is the strong desire of becoming one.

ooo

Early History of Qimancy

The *Book of Odes* is the oldest anthology of poetry in the Chinese tradition. In a cycle of poems praising the exploits of the illustrious ancestors of the Zhou dynasty (1046–256 BCE) the hero Gong Liu appears. The poem recounts the founding of his new domain, and shows him conducting a geophysical survey.

Liu was measuring the shadow of the gnomon, or sundial, to determine the cardinal directions. Sunshine and shade are the original meanings of the well-known terms *Yang* and *Yin*. With this information he could determine which side of the hills and vales received the most sunshine during the winter, as well as the proximity of these sunny dells to sources of water. Such knowledge was crucial for an agrarian tribe that claimed to have descended from the demi-god, Prince Millet.

With these two bodies of evidence – archaeological records of Neolithic China and literary records of legendary China – we can already see the general outline of ancient qimancy (a term denoting 'divination according to *qi*'): The orientation of tombs was as important as the orientation of homes. The minimum requirement for either was the determination of direction. Both astronomical and geophysical factors were consulted. From this originated the two major schools of qimancy, the *Lifa* or Cosmological School (also known as Compass School) and the *Xingfa* or Form School.

The earliest organised school of qimancy was known as *Kanyu*. The locus classicus for this term is the astronomy chapter of the former Han dynasty (206 BCE–220 CE) Daoist text, *Huainanzi*. In it, it is quite clear that some type of astronomical instrument is being manipulated. It may be the *shipan* or cosmograph – an ancient planisphere – that is indicated here, models of which have been discovered in Han dynasty tombs.

The specific meaning of *kan* is *canopy* and that of *yu* is *chassis* – reminiscent of a chariot – in which case the term would mean *heaven and earth* or the *cosmos*. The *School of Kanyu*, therefore, is *cosmic qimancy*. As regards the cosmograph, *kan* would refer to the rotating circular disc – the male component – and *yu* to the square base plate – the female component.

Around both the square and round plates are arranged the names of the 28 constellations of the Chinese zodiac. The 12 months are arranged by decimal number counter-clockwise inside the ring of the heaven disc, while the 12 Earthly Branches – a duodecimal numbering system – representing double-hours of the 24-hour day, occur clockwise on the inner square of the earth plate. In the centre of the disc is a representation of Bei Dou, the Northern Dipper. Moving the disc to the right would represent the rotation of the Big Dipper clockwise around the North Star.

If one observes the southern sky at the same time each night for several nights in succession, the zodiacal constellations will appear to move toward the west. The dial of the cosmograph as it is rotated clockwise on the earth plate corresponds to the arc made by the stars as they pass toward their setting in the west. With the cosmograph the configuration of the heavens could be determined at any time of day or night for any month during the year.

First, the cosmographer would orient the earth board to the cardinal directions, represented by the four sides of the board. Then he would align the number of the month on the heaven disc with the double-hour of the day or night from the earth plate.

Finally, he would note the constellations on the portion of the disc that fronted the southern edge of the board. These are the asterisms that would appear in the sky in the month and hour of the query. In like manner the direction in which the handle of the Dipper is pointing could be determined.

The ancient Chinese believed that the Dipper was the chariot of Shang Di, the supreme deity in the Chinese Pantheon, and the handle represented the focus of his celestial power. Each of the 28 constellations of the zodiac corresponded to a particular earthly region, as did each of the Earthly Branches and, later in the tradition, the eight trigrams of the *I Ching*, the *five elements* or *phases*, etc. Time and space were thus joined in a prognosticatory system that enabled one to choose a fortunate location for a particular time or a fortunate time for a particular location.

The cosmograph is more astrological than geophysical, perhaps, but later accretions would slowly transform it into the familiar luopan, or qimantic compass, of which it is the obvious precursor. The School of Kanyu, therefore, which was one of the first to make use of this proto-compass, is the ancestor of the Lifa School of medieval Chinese qimancy.

Water is the blood and breath (*chi*) of the earth, flowing and communicating as if in sinews and veins. The *Classic of Burial* says: "*Qi* flows where the earth changes shape. The flora and fauna are thereby nourished. It flows within the ground, follows the form of the terrain, and pools where the terrain runs its course. Veins originate in lowland contours; bones originate in alpine contours. They wind sinuously from east to west and from north to south. When thousands of feet distant they are contours; when hundreds of feet nigh they are features. Contours advance and finish in features. This is called total *qi*."

Quoting an earlier text, the *Classic of Burial*, which is now lost, but purportedly dates to the Han dynasty, the relationship of *xing* (form, shape, features) and *qi* are discussed. The *Book of Burial* continues that the proper location of the 'lair', or burial site, is where the 'features finish', and a large portion of the book describes how to recognise these auspicious forms. The dragon and tiger are what protect the district of the lair. On a hill amid folds of strata, if open to the left or vacant to the right, if empty in front or hollow at the rear, life breath will dissipate in the blowing wind.

The *Classic* says: A lair with leakage will harbour a decaying coffin. Here for the first time in the textual tradition the Four Celestial Palaces of the Cerulean Dragon, the Vermilion Bird, the White Tiger, and the Dark Turtle (which originally named the four macro-constellations that compose the ring of the 28 zodiacal constellations) are brought down to earth. On earth these celestial forms delineate the terrestrial forms that occupy the directions of east, south, west, and north, respectively (or left, right, front and back when facing south), of the burial site.

The *Book of Burial* continues: From a passage cited above we learned that "*qi* rides the wind and is scattered, but is retained when encountering water", which was the locus classicus of the term Feng Shui. Here we see that the terrestrial features that block the wind are necessary to prevent the dissipation of the natural flow of *qi* in and along the ground. Flowing water, like wind, also attracts *qi* like a magnet, and the auspicious lair is one that encourages water to linger in its vicinity without stagnating.

The mention of wind and water brings the discussion full circle back to the definition of Feng Shui. The science of Feng Shui in its earliest recorded context specifically refers to the School of Forms. Terrestrial features serve to block the wind – which captures *qi* and scatters it, and channel the waters – which collect *qi* and store it. While Feng Shui may literally indicate *wind and water*, this is merely shorthand for an environmental policy of *hindering the wind and hoarding the waters*. The science of Feng Shui, therefore, is *windbreak-watercourse qimancy*.

The art of *Kanyu*, on the other hand, the precursor of the Compass School, relies strictly on astrology and numerology as a means of fathoming *qi* on a cosmic scale. While Feng Shui is local, *Kanyu* is universal.

Since the medieval period in China – the existence of competing schools notwithstanding – masters of qimancy were versed in the environmental science as well as the occult art. The term, qimancy, divination according to *qi*, applies to both.

Like its sister civilisations in Greece and India, China developed a very sophisticated science of astronomy in its pre-classical period, points out Dr Stephen Field of Trinity University. We have tapped his extensive knowledge of Chinese history to provide readers with a broader and holistic understanding of Feng Shui. Both solar and lunar eclipses are recorded on oracle bones from the mid-fourteenth to the mid-thirteenth centuries BCE, he adds. The most ancient extant record of a nova, or stellar explosion, is also contained in an oracle bone dating to circa 1300 BCE.

The oracle bones also record the names of four stars whose culmination marked the arrival of the solstices and equinoxes. Already in the fourteenth century BCE we see the nucleus of the Four Celestial Palaces, whereby the celestial equator is divided into four equal sections. Although seven constellations on this great circle are mentioned in the *Book of Odes* (ninth century BCE), it is not until the late Warring States period (403–221) that the names of the entire zodiac were recorded.

Ancient Chinese astronomers were fully aware that the quarterly (six-hour) diurnal rotation of the heavens was equivalent to the seasonal (tri-monthly) annual revolution. With knowledge of what star was passing the meridian at sunset, a quick glance at the cosmograph could tell what constellation had culminated at noon or which one would be culminating at midnight.

Or, knowing that a particular constellation had risen at sunset on the vernal equinox, a person would know what constellation was rising, culminating, or setting on the summer solstice.

More importantly, perhaps, the disposition of the Dipper's handle could be predicted. The Dipper was the throne of Shang Di, the High Lord, and the handle indicated the focus of his power.

So what does this ancient cosmology, and particularly the astronomical and astrological cosmograph, have to do with Feng Shui? Those with even a cursory knowledge of Feng Shui will recognise the dragon and tiger as the terrestrial models of the land forms to the east and west, or to the left and right, respectively, of the site being oriented by the Feng Shui master.

In ancient Chinese myth there is the tale of a primordial battle. Previously the circular Heaven was separate from the square Earth and was supported by eight great mountains in each of the eight directions. When the water demon Gong Gong fought with the fire god Zhu Rong, he toppled the north-western pillar, Mount Buzhou, causing Heaven to fall downward and Earth to tilt upward in the north-west. After this catastrophe the rivers of China from that moment onwards flowed south-eastwards, and the stars flew towards the north-west.

It is the ideal world existing before the Great Flood that is captured by the cosmograph. The fact that these instruments were placed in tombs to accompany the deceased in the afterlife attests to their numinous quality. Rather than merely representing the ideal world, the cosmograph was a divine instrument that connected the two realms.

In the ideal world the four celestial deities of the dragon, tiger, bird and turtle do indeed meet the earth as they traverse the horizon. The permanent situation captured on the earth plate of the cosmograph – dragon to the east, bird to the south, tiger to the west, and turtle to the north – represents the spring equinox. In many ancient cultures, including China, this marks the beginning of the new year.

When the Feng Shui master replaced the cosmologist in the centuries during and after the Han dynasty, the cosmograph slowly evolved into the compass, and the function of the instrument evolved from celestial to terrestrial divination. But the purpose was unchanged. The hope was that humans might recapture the perfection of the ideal world. When he locates the dragon and tiger in his local environment, the Feng Shui master has discovered a veritable heaven on earth.

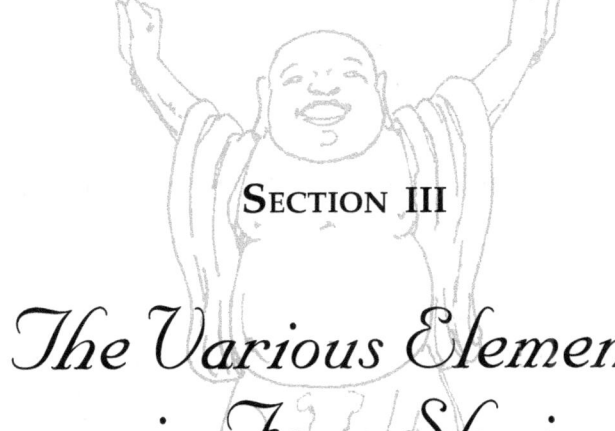

Section III

The Various Elements in Feng Shui

More Hints for Protection

Feng Shui has many protectors and remedies but they should be used with care, common sense and control. If they don't fit into your culture, your temperament, your spirit or your home, it is best to avoid them altogether. For example, crystals and mirrors used thoughtfully benefit the Feng Shui of one's home. Using them carelessly could create problems that did not exist before. Changes have to be made with care. But if things are going great guns for you, it may be counter-productive to make unnecessary changes. Embellishments and additions without reason may only boomerang.

Don't go overboard with mirrors, plants and so on. Think about balance and proportion and the best position for an object in the room. Also choose items that fit with

the style of your home and your own taste. There is no need to use Chinese or oriental-style objects if this is not your style. People travel a lot these days and many homes are filled with bric-a-brac from all over the world. That is different from deliberate, well-intentioned use of Feng Shui items. Whatever you use should fit in well with the theme of the home.

There are a number of remedies for Feng Shui problems in the home. Each one has a specific function. Once the principles are clear, you can use each remedy in a variety of different circumstances.

Lights

Light is a powerful way of activating *chi* both inside and outside the home. It serves to enrich and stimulate *chi*. As light relates closely to fire, it is strongest in the southern part of the house or in the southern part of individual rooms. It also offers good support for the qualities of earth in the south-west and the north-east.

Lights can be used anywhere to energise missing areas of the home or room, dispel stagnant *chi* and generate Yang energies. They are ideal for lighting up the *chi* on sharp edges of furniture. Tall lights can also be used to regularise the shape of the home by re-energising missing corners. Light can be used anywhere where bright energy is required.

Natural light is the best source. So, it is best if rooms have sufficient natural light. Allow the sun to seep in and light up corners. If there isn't enough sunlight, minimise curtains and add mirrors to reflect the light. As we have mentioned several times, it is all a question of balance. If there is too much light in a room, the Yang can be too strong, especially in a bedroom. In that case, curtains can be used to restore the balance in favour of Yin. Active rooms should be more brightly lit than those used for restful occupations. Lights should be clear and bright but never too glaring. Always aim for the right balance in lighting.

Avoid using strong lights directly over people's heads. Lighting should also depend on the activity in the room. For example, a living room may be lively and active during the day and quiet in the evening. So the light in the day can be bright, and more sober or Yin in the evenings.

Candles can also be used to provide light, but remember that it is the actual candle flame that activates the *chi*, not the candle itself. So there is no point in having candles as decorative objects. Use candles in the north-east to activate the earth element, or use them in alcoves or corners to energise stagnant *chi*.

It is usually not a good idea to over-emphasise the fire element in the southern sectors as it can become too predominant. Also, remember that lighted candles can be a fire hazard and so great care should be taken in placing them.

Mirrors

Mirrors attract and pass on *chi* and can be used in a number of ways. Where a section is missing from a house or a room, mirrors can be used to give the effect of the existence of that area, restoring the balance of the house. Mirrors can be used to deflect bad *chi*. They can also allow energy to flow along narrow, constricted passages. By encouraging natural light, mirrors can also help activate and stimulate *chi*.

Another quality of mirrors is that they double the good qualities of the image they reflect. So it is important that they always reflect something pleasant. This makes them ideal for hanging in a dining room where they reflect the food on the table. It is not as good, however, if they reflect food being prepared in the kitchen. Many restaurants have mirrors placed all over. Irani restaurants in Mumbai and Chinese restaurants all over the world are good examples of this.

Mirrors should be used with great care in bedrooms, as it is not good Feng Shui to reflect the bed. This is very important. If a person sleeping is reflected full length in a mirror, he will gradually get debilitated, as he will be unable to have restful sleep. This can lead to health problems. Mirrors should also not reflect the toilet, nor should they reflect the front door as this will encourage the *chi* entering the house to go straight back out again.

Mirrors should be large enough to reflect a complete image, especially of a person, and ideally should allow space around them so that the image is not constrained in the mirror frame. It is not good Feng Shui to have them cutting off the tops of the heads of people in the home. Mirrors should reflect an unbroken image, so mirror tiles or decorated mirrors are not the best Feng Shui, especially if they are reflecting the images of people.

Small, round, convex mirrors reflect and expand *chi* energy and can be used both inside and outside the home. As they reflect an image upside-down, they can be used to remove overbearing images, such as a large neighbouring building, but should not be used where they reflect people.

A Bagua mirror, a mirror within a Bagua octagon with the trigrams on the outside, should only be used outside the house. It usually shows the heaven sequence, which is appropriate for gravesites, so it is not suitable for use inside the home. Use it only outside to deflect bad *chi* away from the house. But a note of caution: the bad *chi* may enter the neighbour's house if it is directly opposite.

Crystals

Crystals are the ultimate symbol of the earth element. They are best used in the south-west, centre or north-east. They are not usually placed in the north. Clear crystals such as quartz are most commonly used, but you can also use raw minerals. Crystals encourage and disperse natural light and therefore have an uplifting effect on the *chi* energies, activating the positive and reflecting it outwards.

Hanging crystals in a window will encourage more light and energy into the room, so they are perfect to energise dull or dark rooms, and to enliven alcoves. If they are also able to move, this is another way of stimulating energies. A faceted crystal in the window of a living room will display a Yang rainbow when the light shines on it, creating great good luck for the occupants and increasing the balance of Yang, particularly suitable in a living room or playroom. As the light from the crystal redirects *chi*, it can also be used to soften bad *chi* on sharp corners of rooms or around sharp-edged furniture.

A solid crystal ball can also be used in an appropriate position to activate specific energies. In the south-west corner or in a living room, it can be used to enhance relationships, in the north-east to stimulate the educational advancement of members of the family, or in the east to encourage successful career prospects.

There are several types and qualities of crystals in the market. Make sure you get the right one.

Wind Chimes

Wind chimes vibrate the air to stimulate and cleanse the *chi* and can reduce negative energy and resolve conflict. To be effective, they must be placed where they will move and therefore ring to give a pleasant, resonating sound. Never buy a set of wind chimes unless you have heard the sound they make. Wind chimes make different sounds. So choose the one you like. Use metal chimes in metal or water areas: north, north-west and west. Use wooden chimes in wood areas: south-east and north-west. The chimes should be hollow in order to channel the *chi* upwards, and the best chimes have six, seven, eight or nine rods.

Place wind chimes in the path of fast-moving *chi* to slow it down as they will moderate the *chi* flow, or hang them at the point where *chi* changes direction in order to smooth its path. Hanging them from a protruding beam will be beneficial in directing the energies correctly.

Chimes can be used to stimulate the luck in particular areas, such as in the west to stimulate the luck of the children of the house or in the south-west to encourage good relationships.

Plants

Plants are living objects that nourish and radiate *chi* and bring auspicious energy. They symbolise life and growth to create a fresh atmosphere. Make sure that they are always kept healthy and adequately watered. If they are flowering plants, consider their colours in relation to the elements you want to stimulate.

Plants can be used to stimulate *chi*, which is at risk of stagnating in corners, and to enliven unused spaces. Sharp leafed plants are more Yang and make *chi* move more quickly. Round-leafed plants have more Yin qualities. Linked with the wood element, they can be very effective in the southern parts of rooms to invigorate the fire element.

As plants are wood elements, avoid placing them in the south-west, centre and north-east, which are earth sectors. The living room and dining room are the best places for plants, and they should only be used sparingly in kitchens and bedrooms.

Cacti and spiky plants are not good if placed too near people and should certainly be avoided in the south-west, as this is the relationship zone. Artificial flowers are less effective, but can still stimulate *chi* if they are kept clean and tidy.

Water

Water features can be used both inside and outside the home in the form of fountains, ponds and aquaria. They are most effective in the north, a water area, or in the east or south-east, wood areas.

Water symbolises money, and if the water feature is an aquarium containing goldfish, it is considered particularly lucky. Keep an odd number of fish, and make sure that one of them is black to absorb any negative energies. Place the aquarium in the south-east to activate your financial good fortune, but make sure that it is always clean and that the water is constantly moving. A stagnant aquarium will have the opposite effect.

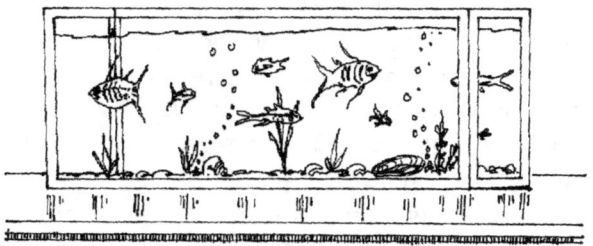

In the north of the living room, one can keep a single bowl of water, perhaps with an image of a turtle, to strengthen the smooth nature of your journey through life.

Paintings of free-flowing, clear water can also be used to stimulate appropriate areas of the house, and can be placed on the left-hand side of the main door to stimulate good luck.

Electrical Objects

In today's world, electrical equipment such as televisions, computers and stereos, to give examples, only stimulate *chi* and these can be placed in specific sites in a room to activate the *chi* energies associated with that area. A television in the eastern section of the living room will stimulate the good health of the family and encourage a positive outlook on life.

But it is a good idea to keep them covered when not in use if they are in the bedroom.

Sound

Background noises can be either annoying or relaxing depending on the character of the noise and the atmosphere of the room. Sound adds life and Yang to a room, so leaving a radio playing can restore the balance to a living room which is too strongly Yin, while it would be unwelcome in a quiet reading room or peaceful bedroom. Match the level of sound to the use of the room and the needs of the occupants.

Common sense is your guide here. Music is also sound and, as we well know, can be healing if it is soft and soothing and mood elevating. Silence can also be interpreted as a different type of sound. Choose your sound.

Screens, Doors and Curtains

Where there is too much *sha chi*, screens can be used to divert the *chi* flow and restore a more favourable balance. They are useful if you have a line of doors through which *chi* rushes too quickly, or to restore a regular shape to a room.

Where *sha chi* is created by an open bookcase, a screen or door over the bookcase will prevent the adverse *sha chi* from affecting the occupants of the room.

Curtains can also be used to soften *sha chi* by eliminating harsh corners and their soft, Yin qualities can help restore a relaxing balance in a room that is too strongly Yang. By blocking out light, they also increase the Yin, which can be used to good effect. Net curtains block out inauspicious views from the windows, while still allowing light into the room. The flow of light can easily be controlled depending on want and need. You will feel the need for more or less *chi*.

Symbols

Appropriate symbols can energise areas of a room. A red rose, for example, can energise your romance corner. If you are using symbolic objects, however, always choose items which are meaningful to you. Do not try to incorporate oriental symbols if they do not fit with your décor or with your own feelings. Fit in what you feel comfortable with and go with the flow. Symbols can be of your choice, but there are certain guidelines in Feng Shui that also use a lot of common sense.

When you are using objects or images, place them in the area of the room or house which you want to stimulate. For example, place a picture of a beautiful landscape in the northern corner of a room to encourage a smooth career path, or a vase of flowers in the south-west to foster good marital relationships.

Some symbols also have an elemental association and, therefore, are best placed in specific areas of the house. Bamboo, for example, is a wood symbol and, therefore, is best used where the qualities of wood need to be supported or stimulated. In other cases, try to use an object which is made of an appropriate substance in the right areas of the house. For example, a metal turtle will be supportive in the northern sector of a room.

You can also relate the symbols to the appropriate numbers relevant to their positions: one metal turtle in the north; two red mandarin ducks in the south-west; three fish in the east.

Symbols also have traditional meanings. The bat is for luck and happiness, butterflies for love and joy, coins for prosperity, fish to ward off evil, jars placed near the entrance encourage *chi* to settle and accumulate, monkey for cleverness and protection from bad luck, eagle for farsightedness, dragon is the ultimate symbol of good luck, horse for speed and perseverance, landscapes stimulate good fortune, oranges are for gold, peacocks for beauty, pomegranates for progeny, peaches for long life, swallows for prosperity and success and so on...

Bamboo Flutes

Bamboo flutes are a potent Chinese symbol, bringing good luck and driving off evil. One way in which they can be used is to dissolve the *sha chi* created by beams in the ceiling. Hang a pair of bamboo flutes on overhead beams at a thirty-degree angle to represent the shape of the top of the Bagua, with the mouthpieces pointing downwards. Using a red ribbon will bring additional good luck.

Pictures

Pictures are very potent symbols. They should always be chosen because they are pleasing – common sense will tell you that – but they can be placed in more or less auspicious positions according to Feng Shui principles.

The images actually displayed may relate to the elements or to things which are particularly symbolic. For example, the ideal place for a picture of a pair of mandarin ducks is in the south-west relationships sector. If you have a picture there of a solitary person walking along a beach, perhaps it might be better to find an alternative position for that image.

Colour

Colour can be used to stimulate, support or negate elemental effects. Colours also have different associations. In the East, red is an auspicious colour which brings happiness, especially with the New Year, while white is associated with mourning. Yellow indicates longevity, blue reflects the sky, and green symbolises growth and freshness.

Your personal element based on your year of birth will also influence your use of colour in the home.

ooo

Feng Shui in the Workplace

As we have seen quite clearly, both Vaastu and Feng Shui have a lot of common sense running through them. The reader may also notice many similarities between the two as both were conceived to better the quality of life. With some knowledge of the science, a good interior decorator can make very positive changes to the house or office.

Both the Form School principles and the Bagua can be applied to any building to assess its most auspicious qualities from a Feng Shui point of view. This is also true of one's workplace, whether it is an office, a studio or any other building. If you are dealing with an entire building, you will need to go through all the relevant stages as you would with a house.

Four Celestial Animals

The optimum position for any building reflects the support of the four celestial animals: the high hills of the dragon on the left; the low hills of the tiger on the right; rounded support from the turtle behind; and broad space with undulations at the front to symbolise the phoenix.

The flow of *chi* should ideally be steady and constant, neither rushing in a destructive fashion nor stagnating in corners. Killing arrows directed at the building by straight roads or angular structures will cut through and debilitate positive energies. The direction of the main door will also influence the fortunes of the building and those working within it.

Floor Plan and Arrangement

By applying the Bagua to the overall floor plan of the offices, you can assess the optimum positions for the employees depending on their particular skills and job responsibilities. Managers in the north-western sector, creative workers in the east, those with financial responsibility in the south-east, and human resources departments in the south-west are ideal placements.

The optimum place for the managing director's office is in the heart of the building, as s/he needs to be in touch with the vital energies of the business. If the room has a high ceiling, it will provide an atmosphere of expansion and success.

If the arrangement of the offices is not as you would wish, look at the elemental qualities of the zones in which particular departments are placed and decide on how to stimulate the qualities which will be most useful to you.

The same principles apply when planning the arrangement and seating positions of the boardroom or a meeting room. If possible, the chairperson of the meeting should be in the north-west sector of the room and facing north-west to enhance his/her capabilities as a responsible and effective leader.

Yin and Yang

Because an office is a place of activity, it is important to ensure that the Yang energies are stronger. Inside the building, the best colours to use are generally fairly neutral, as the level of electrical energy from active people, not to mention computers, printers, photocopiers, telephones and so on, will automatically mean that the atmosphere is Yang.

However, splashes of bright and lively colours in pictures or other smaller features are useful stimulation. This, however, does not apply to rest rooms which need to be as calm as possible and as distant from the noisy ethos of the rest of the office.

Arrangement of Furniture

Furniture arrangement within individual offices should follow the usual principles of aligning with the positive energies of the Bagua and with the most auspicious directions of the person using the space. Even if you cannot align the desk with the best direction, try to avoid the worst ones.

Desks should not be placed in such a way that the occupants have their back to the door. They shouldn't have their backs positioned to the window as well. Otherwise *chi* will enter through the door and go straight out through the window, missing any chance to settle and accumulate. If there is a window behind the desk, keep the blind closed while you are sitting at it. People sitting at desks too close to doors will find that their concentration is easily disturbed as they are too near to the change in the *chi* energies entering the room. In a home, a wind chime would moderate the flow, but if this is distracting, perhaps a plant may help.

People working at desks too near the corner, especially if their chairs are actually in the corner of the room, will be influenced by slow-moving or possibly stagnant *chi* in the corner. Move the desks or stimulate the *chi* with a crystal.

Interior Decoration

Wooden desks are ideal. They offer both support and growth potential. Black-coloured desks are better avoided. Work desks should be comfortably large. Square or rectangular desks offer the support of the earth. Round or semi-circular desks are best for those in creative fields. Reflective surfaces or mirrors near the desk are bad Feng Shui, as they apparently double the amount of work to be done.

High piles of work will also be oppressive to personal *chi*. So keep paperwork and clutter to a minimum. Don't allow paper and files to pile up. They block *chi*. A tidy office, home or workplace is not just common sense. It is essential Feng Shui.

When you are on the telephone, make sure that the cable does not cross the work area and that you are able to sit straight while talking. If you bend your spine and sit with the phone cradled on your shoulder, your spine will not be straight and the flow of personal *chi* will be blocked. You will therefore not perform as effectively when doing business on the telephone. This is more common sense than anything. More such tips will follow.

Lights directly above the head are oppressive to personal *chi* and should be avoided; in fact, try to avoid anything hanging directly overhead as it will have a similar effect. If you cannot move the light, perhaps the desk can be moved slightly. Shelves above the desk also have this effect and are best avoided. Lighting generally should be bright but not harsh.

The colour of the office chairs can be used to stimulate or support the personal element of the person using them. Before that one should have found one's astrological sign and its associated personal element. Metal people should select a brown chair for support or a white one for strength. Water people will find that a blue chair enhances their understanding or a white one will give them strength. A green chair will encourage the co-operative strengths of wood people, while a blue one will give them more understanding in dealings with others. Red chairs will make fire people even more dynamic, although it may be better to choose green to help develop their ability to co-operate with others. Earth people will feel comfortable with the support of a brown earth chair, but may benefit more from the added dynamism of a fire-red chair.

Pictures on the wall, while embellishing the space, can also uplift the mood of the ambience and generate positive energy. The ideal picture to position on the wall behind the desk is one of a mountain to offer the support of the celestial turtle. Images that are abstract or too strong, however, will be a distraction and should be avoided or repositioned.

Directing the Chi Flow

Angular furniture, open bookshelves, filing cabinets, piles of work on desks and in trays – all these can create *sha chi* which cuts through positive energies. Be careful when positioning furniture. Place plants to soften edges and use closed bookcases and cabinets.

Office furniture is generally square or rectangular, shapes which offer sound elemental qualities. If your office furniture features sharp angles or triangles, be especially careful to balance these aggressive fire shapes and to avoid positioning the points to shoot directly at people sitting in the office.

Above all, keep the office as clear of clutter as far as possible. A well-organised and tidy office fosters positive and structured thought and the ability to reason more clearly and effectively. Make sure the dustbin is not in the south-east – a bad position for a dustbin when the controlling energies are relevant to finances.

Plants are also a good way to stimulate areas of stagnant *chi* caused by a blocked-off section of the office if you are unable to rearrange the furniture to allow an easier flow of energies.

Stimulating Specific Areas

There are many ways to stimulate energy in the office. Elemental colours and symbols, lights, crystals, plants or mirrors can work wonders. If working relationships amongst colleagues are troubled, stimulate the south-western zones. Energising the north-west will support and encourage the management team and strengthen their leadership qualities. Lack of creativity can be redressed by activating the western sector, while those looking for fame and recognition should look to the south.

The south-east should always be carefully examined and dealt with in any business. In particular, the south-eastern sector, sometimes known as the fortunate blessings' sector, would benefit from a vase of fresh flowers.

ooo

Understanding the Trigrams

The universe is a balance of Yin and Yang. The balance between the two creates different types of energy. A predominantly Yang energy will be different in quality from a predominantly Yin energy about which we have explained in great detail. These qualities evolve into the five elements that are linked with specific compass directions and with eight divisions of *chi* energy. Each of these divisions is represented by a Chinese name and a trigram – a group of three lines that illustrates its Yin/Yang balance. Each one is also linked with a special member of the family and has a range of inherent characteristics.

"It is essential to understand the characteristics of the energy associated with the eight basic trigrams when beginning to apply Feng Shui to your home. Their qualities can then be used carefully to advantage," says Feng Shui expert Wendy Hobson in *Simply Feng Shui*. She describes the properties in detail.

Chien

Chien is the Yang Trigram that relates to the father or male head of the household and to all men over the age of 46. Its symbol is heaven and it is related to the greater metal element, indicating strength and immobility. Associated colours are gold and silver. The changing season from autumn to winter is indicated by this sector, which is positioned in the north-west.

Kan

Kan is associated with the middle son of the household and men between 16 and 30. It relates to the element water and, therefore, the colours black and blue and the season of winter, which is aligned with the northerly direction. Its symbol is also water. Qualities of this sector's energy involve movement and change.

Ken

Symbolised by a mountain, *Ken* relates to the youngest son in the household, boys up to the age of 15 and the direction north-east. Lesser earth is the relevant element here and the colour yellow. This segment relates to changing seasons, winter moving to spring. Motivation, purpose and knowledge are the strongest energies.

Chen

Positioned in the east, *Chen* is the trigram of the eldest son of the household and men between 31 and 45. Dark green is the colour of the greater wood element here, the season is spring and the symbol thunder. This is an outward-moving energy relating to decision-making and ambition.

Hsun

Related to the eldest daughter and women from 31 to 45, the *Hsun* Trigram is in the south-east. Lighter green and lesser wood are its colour and element. The symbol is the wind. Expanding energies here relate to wealth and the south-east is often known as the fortunate blessings direction.

Li

In the south, the season is summer, symbolised by the sun or by lightning. Red is the colour of this sector, which is linked with the middle daughter or women from 16 to

30. An upward-moving energy resides here, encouraging passion and recognition.

Kun

The Yin symbol of *Kun* relates to the mother of the house and women over the age of 46. In the south-west, it is an earth symbol with the colour brown, associated with late summer. Greater earth is also the symbol of this sector. All maternal qualities apply, including strong relationships, caring and enveloping energies, trust and understanding.

Tui

Tui represents the youngest daughter and girls up to the age of 15. The symbol of this direction is a lake, and it relates to the element lesser metal and the colour white. Relationships are a feature of the energy here, related to children, creativity, joy and romance.

The Bagua

It has already become clear that the elements of Feng Shui are linked together and begin to overlap and interconnect in a variety of different ways. The linking symbol is the *Bagua*, or *pa kua*, which simply means 'grid'. Based on the compass, the trigrams are positioned around the compass points, thus creating a position for the various qualities associated with them.

By using the Bagua on the arrangement of rooms in your home, and on individual rooms, you can optimise the energies within the family.

The Earlier Heaven Sequence

The original arrangement of the trigrams around the compass is known as the earlier heaven sequence. The positions of the trigrams represent the ancient or heavenly order and are used only in the Feng Shui of tombs and finding the optimum position for gravesites.

Chien, the Yang Trigram, is positioned in the south opposite *kun*, the Yin Trigram in the north, as these are opposites. Similarly, *li* in the east is opposite *kan* in the west; *tui* in the south-east opposes *ken* in the north-west and *hsun* in the south-west is opposite *chen* in the north-east.

Thus the arrangement illustrates the perfect symmetry of the ideal, with symbolic opposites balancing each other on the grid. The universal opposites of heaven and earth; the organic opposites of fire and water; the elemental opposites of mountain and lake; and the impulsive opposites of wind and thunder.

The Later Heaven Sequence

It is the later heaven sequence that is used in all Feng Shui relating to homes and offices. So we can focus on that.

The application of the Bagua to your living areas is simple and versatile. Because of the qualities and relationships that are best served by each of the compass directions, you can apply the Bagua to your home, your office or an individual room by overlaying the Bagua onto a plan of the area. This will show you which areas of the home are most suited to particular activities and for particular members of the household.

Divisions of Chi Energy

The *chi* energy in each sector has particular qualities that make it appropriate for certain activities. Applying this in detail to the Bagua arrangement and relating it to your home allows you to access the various qualities of the *chi* energy.

The North-west

The north-west, *chien*, relates to the father of the household and to men over 46. The support of influential people is the most important aspect of luck in this sector.

The main qualities of the *chi* in this zone relate to responsibility, planning and leadership. It is an inward-moving energy creating its own strength and purpose and fostering the characteristics of leadership and organisation. The north-western part of the house is a good place to position the office or bedroom of the main breadwinner of the house.

The North

The independent middle son or men between 16 and 30 relate to the northern sector, *kan*. Water represents the journey of life and is linked to career and the choices you make in relation to how you structure your life's path. It generally has a meandering and stable energy which relates to independence or even solitude.

Tap into that quiet, tranquil energy by using the northern part of the house as the main bedroom, to encourage a stable sex life and a contented relationship. It is also a good position for meditation. So a room which is used for quiet contemplation would be well positioned here. Northern energies are also good for activating positive changes in one's life.

The north-east

Boys up to the age of 15, the youngest sons, are most relevant to the north-eastern sector, *ken*. The search for knowledge is characterised by this area of the house with its strong, sharp and direct energy, quick to change and eager to get its own way.

This is the best area of the house for learning and education; position the bedrooms of the youngest male members of the house here. Students and those wanting to clarify their aims in life will find this a good zone. The energies support decision-making and provide the drive to attain desired goals.

The East

The eastern sector, *chen*, relates to the eldest son and men between 31 and 45. Health is an important aspect of the *chi* energy in this sector, as is developing ambition and realising dreams. The energy is forward-looking and optimistic. Place the studies of the male members of the family in the east, or use it as the kitchen or a hobby room, which will benefit from the active and practical energies.

The South-east

Hsun is the sector of the eldest daughter and women from 31 to 45. Wealth and prosperity are the most important factors in the south-east. The energy is active, but less aggressive than in the east and suited to mature progress. Place the kitchen in the south-east sector, or use the sector for the bedroom or study.

The South

The middle daughter relates to the southern sector, *li*, as well as women from 16 to 30 years. A passionate energy resides here and relates to respect, recognition and fame. The south is a good position for the dining room as well as an office room. As it is a strong and passionate energy, it is also suitable for a bedroom.

The South-west

Kun is the sector relating to the mother of the house and women over 46. Love and happy marital relationships are important factors here. The tranquil energy encourages strong relationships and emotional security. This is the best place to position the living room or the family dining room. It is also excellent for the bedroom, as it will encourage a trusting and loving relationship.

The West

The youngest daughter of the house and girls up to the age of 15 relate to the western sector, *tui*. It is the sector of the house associated with children, creativity, joy and romance. It is good for a dining or living room for a family with children and will encourage a deep and loving family structure. Both children and adolescents with their bedrooms in the west will feel loved and safe.

The Centre

The centre of the Bagua is important for the family, as it is the source of all energies in the house. It is related to the earth and the colours yellow and brown and to the spiritual, emotional and physical health of the family. The centre of the house should be kept clear and uncluttered to allow the free movement of the *chi* energy through the house.

It is a good place for the main room where all members of the family congregate and there is laughter and interaction.

ooo

Activating the Energies in Your Home

In the first place, the question of balance must be addressed, as many people will not have the perfectly regular floor plan that makes for ideal Feng Shui. The house may have been extended and have an additional area jutting out from the main body of the house, or it may have an indent, with part of one or more of the zones missing. Before you can accurately apply the Bagua to your home, eliminate these imbalances.

Property Extensions

Many modern houses have been extended and this means that your floor plan may be irregular. This is common in the bigger cities, as every inch of space is vital. This is not ideal Feng Shui and will have an effect on the nature of the energy in the home because it will cause an imbalance between the different sectors.

If your house has an extension, measure its width along the adjoining wall on your plan. Then measure the length the building extends from that wall. An extension which is less than half as long as the width of the adjoining wall will have a positive effect on the area of the house in which it falls. But extensions larger than this will cause the *chi* to be unbalanced and the corresponding elemental qualities of that portion will be exaggerated.

Because the qualities of the *chi* energies in each sector relate to individuals, they may influence one member of the family more than another. Because the energies are associated with the elements, those qualities are also relevant and are used to redress any imbalances.

Extensions in the North-west and West

Small extensions in the north-west and west are good for the occupants as they relate to the element metal. This should encourage a steady build-up of career prospects and advantages gained through influential contacts. In the north-west, the benefit will primarily be reaped by the older men in the family and those in positions of responsibility.

Activate the water element in the extension to reduce the effect of the overabundance of metal. Use black or dark blue in the décor or in ornaments or paintings. For example, hang a blue-framed or black-framed mirror on the west or north-west-facing wall. Yellows and browns will support the metal still further, so avoid these colours, ceramic objects and any earth symbols, as well as metal colours or objects.

Extensions in the South-west and North-east

Small extensions in the north-east encourage good motivation and are good for students. In the south-west, a small extended area will give support to the cohesion of the family.

Where the earth element is over-emphasised in these areas by a large extension, it can lead to selfishness and greed. Domestic and health problems may occur. Use white to modify the excessive effects of earth in these areas. Mirrors with gold or silver frames can be hung on the south-west or north-east-facing walls. Generally, stimulate the metal element to recreate a more even balance. Keep away from earth colours and symbols. Fire energy supports earth. So avoid red colours, candles or other fire symbols.

Extensions in the South

In the south, small extensions will encourage a sociable outlook, a good circle of friends and perhaps even public recognition. If this fire area is stimulated too much, volatile emotions, stress and tensions of all kinds, including health problems, will result.

Calm the passion of fire with earth symbols. Use yellow or brown colours in the décor and hang a mirror on the south-facing wall to deflect the energies. Avoid using too much wood, which would feed the fire, but choose ceramics and earth symbols to stimulate the earth element. Reds and oranges are also best left out of the extension.

Extensions in the South-east and East

Harmonious relationships and financial good fortune are associated with small extensions in the south-east. The south-east will particularly benefit the eldest daughter or son.

Larger structures will create an imbalance in the wood element, which will result in numerous problems. Fire will burn off the excessive strength of the wood element. So use reds and oranges, and hang a mirror on the south-east or east-facing wall, preferably with a red frame. Avoid blue, green and water symbols.

Extensions in the North

In the northern sector, small extensions will encourage independence and a steady advancement along the career path. If the water element is thrown out of balance by a large extension in the north, one may feel overwhelmed and drowned by problems.

Activate wood to absorb the water. Use plants to decorate the extension. Green colours will be beneficial, as well as wooden furniture or ornaments. Don't add more blue or black, and keep away from white, silver and gold, the metal colours or symbols that enhance the wood qualities.

Missing Sections of a Property

Similarly, if the shape of the house shows an indented section, or an extension creates an overall shape in which a particular section is missing altogether, the situation will need to be rectified. Whether an extension is creating an imbalance or a section is missing, the aim is to recreate a regular shape, either actually or symbolically, thereby giving each sector its proper balance. If you can re-establish a regular shape by building an extension to regularise the shape of the house, it is ideal.

It should be remembered that since the energy directions are also associated with parts of the body, missing sections of the house can relate to illnesses or health problems in those physical areas.

Sections Missing in the North-west and West

If the north-western or western zones are missing, then metal is out of balance. Weakness of character may result, as well as a breakdown of communication. The north-west will particularly affect the fortunes of the father or the major breadwinner in the family. The west may have more effect on the children and make them feel unstable and possibly unloved. Respiration or elimination problems become more likely.

If you paint the walls around the extended area white or place mirrors on the north-west or north-facing walls, this will give the illusion of a complete area. Use round metal shapes for the mirrors and other furniture, if possible.

Sections Missing in the South-west and North-east

When the earth section is depressed, there will be a feeling of insecurity. Disturbed sleep and poor nourishment are symptomatic of missing earth zones. Paint the walls around the missing sections in yellows or browns and use square-shaped furniture or mirrors on the walls, preferably with brown or yellow frames. Avoid the use of reds or oranges.

Sections Missing in the South

A home sans the southern section of the house will result in a debilitated social life. Health will also be affected. South-facing walls are best painted in fairly strong fire colours, or use rugs or small ornaments in reds and oranges or even purple. Pictures should be chosen with the support of the fire element in mind.

Sections Missing in the South-east and East

Zones of the house missing from the south-eastern portion are not good for the financial health of the family. A missing eastern section will adversely affect the health of the family. Bolster the wood element with green colours, well-tended plants and mirrors with green frames on the south-east or east-facing walls. Blue in small quantities can give additional support.

Sections Missing in the North

This mainly affects the men and their career prospects. Sexual problems are the most likely health risk along with illnesses affecting the kidneys or poor elimination. Blue walls will help activate the missing water energies, with a mirror on the north-facing wall preferably with a black frame. A water feature, such as a small aquarium, could be placed against the wall.

Use Both Internal and External Space

It is possible to use the exterior to activate missing corners. This can be done in addition to measures taken inside the house. One way is to install a light in the missing corner of the plot, as this will serve to energise the elemental qualities outside the house. Another way is to landscape the area with plants and garden furniture so that it looks like an outside room. Both methods help restore life to the part of the house which was 'missing' from the regular plan.

About activating the plan, Feng Shui expert Wendy Hobson says, "Go back to your floor plans or draw them out again. Centre the Bagua over the plan so that the compass sectors are as evenly balanced as possible and the centre is positioned over the heart of the home. Align the Bagua correctly with the compass directions. Think about how you are going to rebalance the elements, activate any missing sections and reduce dominant qualities in extensions or awkward shapes. Then think about the existing uses of the rooms and consider whether they are ideal in relation to the Feng Shui information you have learned. Concentrate on the activity most often undertaken in that room.

"If the allocation is not ideal, can the use of the rooms be changed? This is sometimes possible, particularly with the allocation of bedrooms. For example, if the bedroom in the west is used by a young man who is just starting university, while his younger brother has his room in the north-east, it might be advantageous to both of them to exchange rooms.

"Clearly for many people, the position of rooms will be fixed, especially for kitchens and living rooms in most houses. In that case, you need to consider how to make the best use of the energies available in the rooms. To do this, you simply apply the Bagua to the room itself rather than to the overall floor plan; you can then stimulate the particular sections of the room most suited to the use of the room itself."

ooo

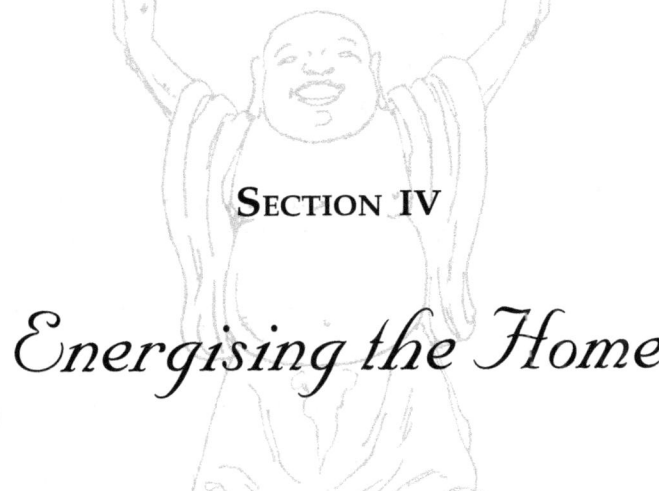

Section IV

Energising the Home

Using Feng Shui in the Home

The process is simple and you can work through many stages. First, make a room plan. Then align the plan with the correct compass direction.

Tidy up the room for starters. Rooms have to be neat and tidy. Clutter discourages the free flow of *chi*. If the room is irregular in shape, try to compensate for the missing areas. Position the furniture in the most auspicious section of the room to align them with the right directions for good luck. Always make sure that *chi* flows gently and easily through the room. Also, make attempts to balance the Yin and Yang. Every section of a room has energy. If necessary, stimulate particular areas to bring the necessary changes in your life.

Make sure that symbols and colours in each sector are appropriate to the dominant element. As required, stimulate or soften the effects of the elements within the room. Use the principles of Feng Shui to check if the room is appropriate for the person who uses it.

The entrance of the house is very important. *Chi* enters through the main door and moves through the home. The best entrance halls are wide enough to allow the *chi* to settle and accumulate. All halls should be kept clear and tidy. Otherwise they will encourage stagnant *chi*.

The entrance hall should have an even balance of Yin and Yang both in the décor and the lighting. Doormats can be used to welcome the *chi* into the house. Choose a colour that suits the direction in which the door faces. Some Feng Shui practitioners recommend placing three gold coins under the mat to usher good fortune. Choose the Chinese coins that have a hole in the centre and tie them together with lucky red ribbons. Another tip is to have a bright light just inside and outside the main door. It is also supposed to bring good luck.

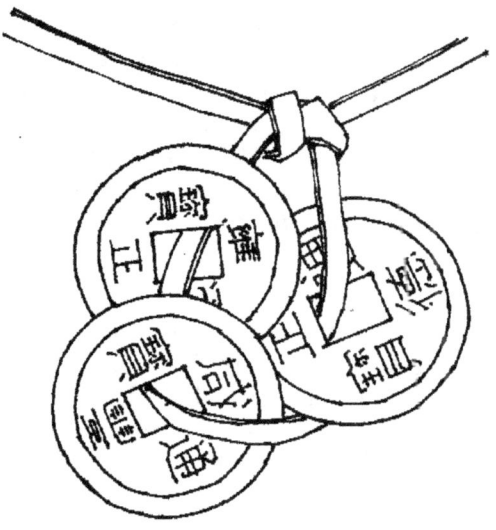

If the halls are long and narrow, place mirrors alternately along the walls so that the *chi* is reflected from side to side and moves in a zigzag route rather than rushing straight down. Plants placed along the sides of the hall will encourage the *chi* towards it. Crystals also help. If they are placed in the centre of the hallway, they will speed up the *chi* flow.

If there is a spiral staircase in the house, hang a wind chime at the top and bottom of the stairs to moderate the flow. Stairs should ideally have solid steps to keep *chi* from frittering its energy. If there is a toilet door near the main door, make sure it is always locked.

The Living Room

The living room must have the right Feng Shui atmosphere as it is the heart of the home and, in some senses, the heart of the family too. To begin with, the shape of the room should be regular. Make sure that there are no obstructions to the free flow of *chi*. Crystals, mirrors and plants can be used to nourish stagnant *chi*. Bamboo flutes tied with red ribbons on the beams help dissipate negative *chi*. If the ceiling is uneven or has beams across it, the free flow of *chi* in the room can be disrupted.

Furniture should also be placed to encourage the free flow of *chi*. Sofas and chairs shouldn't have their backs to the door. It is always good to face the door. Keep the central area of the room free from clutter. Fresh flowers in the living room are a good embellishment. They look good and also nourish *chi*. Open bookcases, if any, can be covered.

In a living room, with all its activity, the Yin-Yang balance is always in favour of Yang. But the right colours, lights, curtains and other devices can create the right balance. Electrical equipment like televisions and stereos will also stimulate the Yang element. Position them carefully. The north and north-west are good places to position them.

The elements are also important in relation to the colour and the objects placed around the room. Wooden objects will enhance growth potential in the south-east. Water symbols will add support to the element. Excess red in the west or north-west is negative, as it will lead to tension in the household. If there is an excess of blue and black in the northern sector, it can drag the energies down. An aquarium can be placed in the south-east and plants in the east. All colours used should be in harmony with the elemental associations in the room.

To perk up one's social life, energise the southern sector with a crystal, lights or some symbolic object. All images hung on the wall should be chosen with care because they can influence one's life. A vase of fresh flowers can energise the living room. Bright flowers in the south are ideal. Interestingly, clocks on the wall can also stimulate areas with their energy and movement.

In modern planning and also due to the crush on space, the open plan room is in vogue, which combines the living and dining areas. But it is important to make a separation between the two functions. Otherwise, neither room will be complete and certain areas of *chi* energy will be lost.

The Kitchen

In a manner of speaking, the kitchen governs the wealth of the family. If the energy levels in the kitchen are balanced, the food prepared will also be balanced and nutritious. The best positions for the kitchen are in the east, south-east or north of the house.

To begin with, the kitchen door should open smoothly and easily to ensure maximum and smooth energy flow. The kitchen is rooted in the water element and symbolises wealth and should therefore be kept spotlessly clean. The kitchen shouldn't be cramped either and the person cooking should have a clear view of the door. The oven should not be in the northern part of the room or in the north-western sector. The north is the ideal zone for the sink. All kitchen appliances should run smoothly, without noise, and without disturbing *chi*.

The fridge is best placed in the south-eastern wealth sector or in the south-west to encourage family relationships. The south is not a good direction for the fridge. Smaller electrical items like kettles can be used in different areas to ensure *chi* stimulation throughout these areas. The kitchen is a scene of activity and so its atmosphere will be Yang. Wood favours Yin, while metal emphasises Yang and so try to achieve a balance between the two. Lights are important in the kitchen but there is no substitute to natural light. Allow as much natural light to enter. If the kitchen is small and dark, the walls can be painted in light colours and artificial lighting can be used.

Plants or a crystal on the windowsill can energise the room. The best plants to grow in the kitchen are fresh herbs as they bring in a lot of positive energy. It is also important to keep the kitchen separate from the dining room. Screens, with two plants at the meeting point, can help. It is necessary for the kitchen, like with the other rooms, to have independent *chi*.

The Dining Room

Good Feng Shui is vital for the dining room as eating well is a social experience. The family bonds at the dining table and the dining room require the right vibrations for it. The ideal position for the dining room is the centre of the house. The room should preferably be well demarcated, spacious and have an easy air about it. Mirrors and dim lights are useful embellishments.

The balance in the dining room should be slightly in favour of Yin. The colours in the room should be muted and not too jarring. The dining table should also be carefully chosen. Space at the table gives a feeling of abundance. Wood is a good choice for the dining table as it has a strong Yin quality to it. Simple-shaped crockery is the best. Metal cutlery can be polished to stimulate *chi* energies. The colour of the table linen should also be chosen with care: blue in the north, green in the east, for example. Crystal glassware is excellent because it activates the *chi* energy. Choose round tablemats for a round table and rectangular ones for a rectangular table.

The plants in the dining room should not be spiky. They should be gently rounded. Flowers of the right colours can stimulate the *chi* on the table. A small aquarium with small, active fish is well suited but it should not be in the southern fire sector. Clocks are better kept away from the dining room, as their constant movement indicating the passage of time may not be conducive to relaxed eating. Soft, instrumental music is always therapeutic. Eating can be made a beautiful and sensuous experience with just a little attention to detail.

Seating is also important. The most important person or the head of the family should be seated at the head of the table, preferably facing the door. The mother in the south-west, if the father is the head of the family. If some other guest is the guest of honour, then the father can be in the north-west, sons in the east, north and north-east and daughters in the south-east, south and west.

The Study

The study is an important part of the home. It can be located in the south-west, which dominates wealth, in the north, which enhances the career, in the north-west, which helps leadership, and in the north-east, which is for knowledge. One can also activate the appropriate elements: metal for strength, earth for knowledge and wood for ambition.

Special zones in the room can also be stimulated using lights and crystals and by placing computers and other electrical equipment in the right places. The energy balance in the study should be in favour of Yang. The room should be well lit. It is even better if there is good natural light. Light activates the surrounding energies.

It is good if the person using the work desk has a clear view of the door. Avoid facing a blank wall. An attractive landscape picture will help escape the feeling of being blocked in. One can also choose the area with the right energy. If the room is small and you can't face the door, a mirror can be hung on the opposite wall.

Avoid angular furniture and open bookshelves. Keep them covered. Remove all clutter. Office spaces and desks can get untidy and can accumulate bad energy. Crystal paperweights and plants can help dispel *sha chi*.

The Bathroom and Toilet

The bathroom, interestingly, also relates to the family finances. The best positions for the bathroom are the east and the south-east. If the water element is too strong, it can be diffused with plants. The bathroom should be clean and airy with the right fragrance. It shouldn't feel dark or cramped. There should be natural light. Mirrors can be used to make it more spacious.

Since the toilet is regularly flushed, remember that it flushes away properties of the zone in which it is placed. The best position for the toilet, therefore, is in the least auspicious direction of the main member of the household or in an area where there is an excess of an energy, which needs to be counterbalanced. Crystals can also be used effectively in the bathroom.

The flushing away of positive energies in the south can lead to a poor reputation; in the north to a lack of career advancement; in the east to bad health; in the west to a lack of romance; in the north-east to low motivation; in the north-west to lack of responsibility; in the south-east to money problems; and in the south-west to poor marital relationships. Therefore, the positioning of the bathroom is very important.

The lid of the toilet and the bathroom door should always be kept shut. Otherwise, the *chi* will be spoilt as it enters the rest of the house. Toilets bring a strong Yin influence to the surroundings and so Yang elements are necessary as a counterbalance. There should be good air circulation and so the bathroom should be well ventilated.

Like with all the other rooms, use common sense and Feng Shui principles to keep the bath and toilet areas clean, fragrant and a happy place to be, even if it is used only for short periods.

The Bedroom

Bedrooms are important to recharge for the challenges of the next day. A good night's sleep is so essential. Bedrooms should therefore be carefully aligned with the right energies. The positioning of the bedroom is vital. The north is ideal for quiet sleep as the zone has a calming energy. The north is also associated with sex and so the bedroom in this zone can be a good place for lovers. The north-east has a sharp, competitive *chi* energy, which can be too strong for bedrooms. It can induce nightmares. The north-west is the best place for parents. The east, with its active and ambitious energies, is ideal for those setting out on their careers with many hopes, dreams and aspirations. The south-east is also a positive position for those looking at a career seriously but it is a bit subtler.

The south is the area of passion and if the bedroom is placed in this direction, the sex life of the occupants will get stimulated. So it is not the best direction for sleep and relaxation. The south-west is rather staid and can create a feeling of caution. So it is not a great direction for the energies of young people to be harnessed.

It is not a good idea to have a bedroom above the garage, as it can be very unsettling. The occupant will have to stimulate the earth symbols to provide support. It is also considered bad luck to sleep in a bedroom above a kitchen. A bedroom in the basement will have an excess of Yin and so it is imperative to add more of the Yang element. If the staircase is facing a bedroom door, hang a wind chime where the energies meet to moderate the flow. It is also not good Feng Shui if the bedroom door is immediately opposite the main door.

Square earth shapes are the best for the bedroom as they have the right Yin energy. Yin should predominate in a place of relaxation. So, to set the mood, use softer colours, dimmer lights and soft furnishing. Plants in the room should be round leafed. Furniture should be rounded too. Tables must also have rounded corners. The bedroom should be in the best position for the occupant. If the room is not in the best location, you can make amends by positioning the furniture properly. The head of the bed can be positioned towards the best relationship direction. Place the bed in the optimum sector of the room and face the right direction when sleeping.

The position of the bed is important. The person using the bed should have a clear view of the door and should not sleep with the feet pointing directly at the bedroom door. Feng Shui practitioners feel that this could result in death, especially if the door leads to a bathroom or toilet. The feet pointing towards the window is also considered bad luck. The bedroom should ideally have only one door to allow the *chi* to enter and flow without obstruction. If there are two doors, shut one. The bed should also not be directly placed between two doors as it may negatively affect the *chi* movement. Beds can be repositioned according to need and the principles of Feng Shui. Screens can also be used effectively.

It is good to have a solid wall behind the bed, as it will offer security. If it is under a window, the person may feel very insecure. If there is no choice to escape the window, make sure that the curtains are drawn. Overhead beams above the bed are also bad *chi* – one should cover these and move the bed as far away as possible from them. Feng Shui practitioners recommend hanging two bamboo flutes at a forty-five degree angle by red ribbons on the beam as a curative measure.

Mirrors play a very important role here. They are often used to give the illusion of more space and to increase the level of light. But mirrors should never reflect the bed. That will be detrimental to the person's health and to personal relationships. The shape of the headboard can also be important. As a tip, curved, metal-shaped headboards are good for office and business workers; rectangular wood-shaped headboards are good for those in the professions; water-shaped headboards for creative types, and so on.

Soft lighting in the bedroom will enhance the Yin qualities of relaxation. Harsh overhead lights are not a good idea. Shelves and cupboards around the head of the bed can also be a problem by blocking the general good fortune. Feng Shui practitioners recommend placing six gold coins on each side of the bed as an antidote. Water features like aquariums are also best avoided in the bedroom.

Yin is for restful sleep. But if one wants to activate one's sex life, the room should have more of the Yang element. The southern part of the room can also be stimulated with red, candles and with a crystal hanging in the window. The stimulation of the western and south-western sectors will help love and romance. Feng Shui practitioners recommend a pair of Mandarin ducks in that zone, which is a symbol of true love.

Children's rooms will obviously have a different energy and will quite naturally tend to be more Yang. Keep the room free of clutter. The north-east is a good energy to enhance and a crystal in the window to catch the light can stimulate the energy of success. A globe or a map of the world can be placed in the north-east sector. Trophies won at school can be displayed in the west or north-west for added strength.

ooo

The Kua Number

Specific compass directions have positive or negative implications for particular members of the family. Each person has compass directions, which are auspicious or inauspicious for him or her. It is easy to calculate one's personal *kua* number or lucky number, based on one's year of birth. Based on your *kua* number, four of the compass directions and locations will be auspicious for you, and four will not.

To calculate your personal lucky number, add together the last two digits of your year of birth. Remember that if your birthday falls between 20 January and 20 February, you must check whether to use the actual year or the previous year. If the total is ten or more, add them together again so that you have a single digit. If you are a man, subtract that number from ten to find your personal lucky number. If you are a woman, add five to the number. If this creates a two-digit number, add those digits together to find your lucky number.

For example, if Naresh was born in June 1966, his lucky number will be 3 – 6 plus 6 makes 12; 1 plus 2 makes 3; then subtract 3 from 10. If Shankutala was born in December 1969, her number will be 2. This is how one arrives at it: 6 plus 9 is 15; 1 plus 5 is 6; 6 plus 5 is 11, and 1 plus 1 is 2.

In the twenty-first century, the calculation is different. Males born in 1999 will have a *kua* number of one; females will have a *kua* number of five. Men born in the year 2000 will have a *kua* number of nine and females a *kua* number of six. Add together the last two digits until you have a single digit. Men should then deduct that number from nine for their *kua* number. Women should add four to their single-digit number.

Once you have discovered your *kua* number, you will be able to determine whether you are an east-group or a west-group person.

East-group people have a *kua* number of one, three, four or nine. Their best directions and locations are north, east, south-east and south; their worst are south-west, west, north-west and north-east.

West-group people have a *kua* number of two, five, six, seven or eight; their best directions and locations are north-east, south-west, west and north-west. Their worst directions are north, east, south-east and south.

According to Feng Shui expert Wendy Hobson, "Although the same four directions are good and bad for all east-group people and all west-group people, the type and degree of good or ill fortune associated with those directions is different for the different *kua* numbers. The four auspicious directions are: *fu wei, tien yi, nien yen* and *sheng chi*. The four inauspicious directions are: *ho hai, wu kwei, chueh ming* and *lui sha*.

"*Fu wei* luck will bring you reasonable good fortune and relates in particular to your personal growth and development. *Tien yi* luck is sometimes known as the good doctor as it relates to your health. *Nien yen* luck specifically refers to your progress in personal relationships, both with family and friends and with romantic partners. *Sheng chi* luck is the most positive direction and should bring overall success and prosperity to your life.

"On the negative side, *ho hai* luck is likely to find you dealing with problems and accidents in your life and suffering frustration in trying to solve them. *Wu kwei* luck, the five ghosts as it translates from the Chinese, is a quarrelsome direction likely to encourage difficult and confrontational relationships. The six killings or *chueh ming* luck is a general bad-luck direction, although the worst direction is *lui sha* or total loss."

Once the personal lucky number is established, it can be used in many ways to maximise the effects of any good luck coming one's way. The main door of the house can face an auspicious direction. The main rooms of the house can be in the best sectors, and the lucky sectors of rooms can be used with profit.

Also, if both partners have the same number they will be compatible in terms of the auspicious directions. This is a simplistic explanation. The intricacies have to be worked out.

ooo

Feng Shui in the Garden

Use the principles of Feng Shui to create an ideal garden. The garden should have the right balance of energies where one can be active and relaxed at the same time. What is essential is to achieve a natural landscape.

"The higher, dragon hills should be on the left of the house, with the lower, tiger hills on the right," says Wendy Hobson. "A rounded hill, building or trees behind will add the support of the turtle, while a spacious area at the front leading to the footstool of the phoenix completes the picture. Ideally, the land behind the house should be higher than that at the front. If landscape features or buildings are not already in place, think about adding trees at the back or to the left of your house, with smaller shrubs to the right and an open area at the front. Do not make the mistake of planting too close to the house and overwhelming the property with shade."

Make sure you don't block off all the natural sunlight coming into the house, as it is the most vital energy.

Dragons never live in completely flat land. So a garden with ups and downs is more beneficial from the point of view of the luck, which the plot can bring into your life. In addition, it will also help create an auspicious circulation of *chi*, making sure that it does not rush across the garden without the chance to meander, settle and accumulate.

Even if the plot is quite small, you can still artificially create small hills and hollows to encourage the smooth flow of *chi*. Small hillocks, rockeries and so on will aid the circulation of *chi*. These will also provide the garden with an exquisite look. If the garden is very steep, *chi* will move downhill. Terraces in the garden will retard the downhill flow of *chi*. Fencing and shrubs can be used to deflect negative energies from outside. Use trailing plants to soften any harsh edges on the property.

The garden is no different from the rooms of the house. Use the same principles for proper energy flow. Rounded, flowing shapes are good Feng Shui. Sharp angles, large flat expanses, corners and swift changes of direction are not as auspicious. Tiny corners or pockets where the *chi* can stagnate will also cause you to lose the benefit of the energies in the garden. Make sure you encourage the *chi* to drift slowly but surely around the garden.

The heights of various trees and shrubs will make a big difference to the *chi* flow around the garden; taller trees or shrubs will act as more effective barriers, while lower-growing ground cover will have less of an effect. Trailing plants soften the edges and create a beneficial effect.

Curved pathways with bricks or stones add flavour to the garden and also help the flow of *chi*. A curved path on the eastern side of the house will activate the dragon and bring good luck. Surround the path with flowering plants for added energies.

Healthy, growing plants give off Yang energy, while anything in the garden that is dead will give off Yin energy. Tend the garden regularly and keep it tidy and healthy. Plants with sharper leaves and lighter foliage have more Yang energy, while plants with rounded leaves have more Yin. Yin plants will also prefer shaded or damper areas, while the Yang plants will prefer the bright areas. Mix foliage, colours and textures, shapes and heights for the best effects. Attempt a garden with the right balance of light and shade. It should look attractive, creative and interesting, with personality, balance and the right positive energy in continuous flow.

Flowering plants bring powerful energy to the garden. They look good, provide adornment to the garden akin to pieces of jewellery, can be planted throughout the year, and can be used to stimulate particular areas, which need increased energy levels.

According to Feng Shui practitioners, red flowers in the southern zone will stimulate passionate energies and encourage your social life. If you are looking for a smoother career path, blue flowers in the northern sector will help, but enliven and strengthen it with white as well. White flowers in the west will help realise one's dreams. Fragrant flowers have wonderful emotional effects and can be very healing to personal *chi*. Plant them near the door of the house and make the most of their healing fragrances. They also look good and lend the garden colour and beauty.

Herbs can also add fragrance, colour and a variety of leaf shapes to the garden. They are also useful in the kitchen and can be used for their medicinal properties. Feng Shui also uses herbal aromas in the house. They are very relaxing and therapeutic.

Basil is said to promote individuality and good fortune in personal ventures. Plant it in the northern area of the garden to encourage strength in your career. Bergamot is an appetite suppressant and lifts the spirits. Plant it in the southern area to improve your standing among friends. Plant camomile in the west or south-west for good family relationships. A vase of freshly picked camomile in the east will help calm those with nervous problems. Camomile tea is also soothing. Dill is said to promote sleep. The northern zone is a good position for this plant. Eucalyptus clears the head, either from head colds or muddled thinking. Plant it in the north-east to promote general clarity of thought and mental awareness.

Jasmine can lift the spirits of those who are depressed and can also encourage good marital relations. Plant it in the sector of the garden that needs stimulation: the east to help the health of the family; the south-west to improve family relationships; and the south-east to encourage financial luck. Juniper in bedroom windows ensures marital happiness.

Lavender has many benefits. It makes a wonderful relaxant and aid to restful sleep, and can be used to help heal burns and soothe sunburn or irritated skin. It will benefit any area of the garden. Mint promotes good memory and is refreshing. A good place to plant mint is in the north-eastern part of the garden to help in your search for knowledge or enlightenment. Thyme should be planted in the south-eastern corner to promote wealth, or in the north to encourage a good career. In the home, it can be used to lift depression. Rosemary is said to improve the memory. Plant it in the south-west to encourage remembrance between old friends.

Ponds, waterfalls, streams, fountains and birdbaths add character, variety and energy to the garden. The best compass sectors for water features are the north, south-east and east sectors as these are related to water and wood. It is essential that the water remains clear and preferably flowing, as this will bring good luck. Stagnant to dirty water, as we have repeatedly mentioned, is not good Feng Shui.

If you are building a pond, choose a curved shape, which relates to natural shapes and fits in with the general meandering nature of the garden. Kidney or crescent shapes, especially if they are curving towards the house, are very auspicious. If the shape curves away from the house, add some garden lights on the furthest points to redirect the energies back towards the house. Don't be tempted to make the pond too large for the proportions of the garden. You could then feel swamped by the water qualities you have created. If the pond is too large, increase the light around it and add a rock garden or some boulders around it to rebalance the space.

Keep some fish in the pond, especially goldfish, choosing an odd number. Replace them if they die, as they will have absorbed your bad luck. Toads are also good luck. So they should be encouraged to live in your pond.

Swimming pools in residences are not good Feng Shui because they create large water bodies disproportionate to the size of the house. They can have the effect of overwhelming the house. Locate the pool in the north or in the lowest part of the plot. Try to screen it from the house with trees or shrubs to diminish any adverse effects.

Always keep larger trees and shrubs well pruned. Plants that are brown or dying will give off excessive Yin energy and create an imbalance in the energies.

Garden lighting, apart from energising stagnant areas of the garden, will add to your good luck especially if they are placed around the boundaries of the plot. A light in the southern corner of the garden, which is switched on for a few hours each day, will bring good luck to the family by stimulating the fire zone. For stable and loving marital relationships, place a light in the south-west sector; for romance, select the west.

If you have decorative statues, garden furniture or urns to landscape your garden, think about the element from which they are made before placing them in an appropriate zone of the garden. Ceramic urns or pots of plants will bring you the best luck if they are placed in the earth sectors – south-west or north-east – or in the metal sectors – west or north-west. Wooden garden furniture will be best positioned in the east, south-west or south. Metal objects will be best in the west, north-west or north.

Boulders add stability to life. Place them in the earth sectors – south-west or north-east. For strength of purpose, place them in the west or north-west. If there are barbecues in the garden, they should stimulate the fire element and should be placed in the south, south-west or north-east.

ooo

Glossary

Bagua	=	Linking symbol or grid
Chen	=	Wood trigram
Chi	=	Cosmic energy (*prana*)
Chien	=	Hard metal trigram
Hsun	=	Relating to expanding energies
I Ching	=	*Book of Change*
Kan	=	Relating to the water element
Kanyu	=	Feng Shui's predecessor science
Ken	=	Relating to changing seasons
Kua	=	Lucky number based on year of birth
Kun	=	Yin symbol relating to maternal qualities
Li	=	Upward moving energy; fire trigram
Lo pan	=	Chinese compass
Lo shu	=	Magic square
Qi	=	Variation of *chi*
Ren chai	=	Luck one creates on earth
Sha	=	Bad or negative influence
Sha chi	=	Negative *chi*
Sheng chi	=	Life breath; force that controls destiny
Tai chi	=	Source of all energies
Ti chai	=	Earth luck
Tien chai	=	Heaven luck
Trigram	=	Group of three lines illustrating Yin-Yang balance
Tui	=	Soft metal trigram
Xing	=	Form, shape or features
Yao	=	Bit
Yang	=	Masculine force
Yin	=	Feminine force

Note : *The meanings of Chinese terms given above are in the specific context of this book. In some instances, in another context the words could have other connotations.*

www.ingramcontent.com/pod-product-compliance
Lightning Source LLC
Chambersburg PA
CBHW070334230426
43663CB00011B/2316